PRAISE FOR *LABOR'*

"One of the untold stor
over the past ten years h
progressive Service Employees International Union into a twenty-
first-century version of business unionism, its leaders allied to
corporate and neoliberal interests from both major political
parties. Cal Winslow offers a unique glimpse into this heartbreak-
ing tragedy and how rank-and-file workers are fighting back."
— **Juan Gonzalez, New York *Daily News***
columnist and co-host of *Democracy Now!*

"The civil war inside the SEIU is a tragic story. Yet, as Cal Winslow
emphasizes in this urgent and dramatic account, it may contain
the seeds of authentic renewal in the American labor movement."
— **Mike Davis, author of *City of Quartz* and *Planet of Slums***

"NUHW's fight for rank-and-file, militant, and democratic unionism against SEIU is the most important battle taking place in the
labor movement today. Read this book to get the story and learn
why a victory for NUHW would be victory for all workers."
— **Robert Brenner, author of *The Economics***
of *Global Turbulence*

"The NUHW leadership and staff have fought valiantly over the
years to win the highest standards in wages, benefits, and quality
representation for workers both on the job, in the community
and in the legislature. Having worked with them for many years
and witnessed their courageous struggle, I honor their important
movement to maintain the honesty and integrity of their democratic labor organization as the newly named NUHW. This book
has a lot of valued lessons for all who yearn for justice for working
people. I urge everyone to read it."
— **Dolores Huerta, first vice president *emerita***
and co-founder, United Farm Workers

"The emergence of NUHW has been one of the most exciting recent developments in U.S. labor. From the ashes of the old, healthcare workers in California are trying to build something that's new, different, and definitely worth fighting for. Cal Winslow's account of their difficult struggle is moving and insightful—and maybe even a roadmap for others to follow."
— **Steve Early, labor activist and journalist, author of *Embedded with Organized Labor***

"The birth of NUHW signals a time of momentous transition not just for healthcare workers but for all workers in this country. Winslow tells the story. It is a wake-up call for everyone interested in the future of American labor."
— **Mike Casey, president, UNITE HERE Local 2 and president, San Francisco Labor Council**

"If ever there was a need for a combative, principled workers' movement, it's now—which makes SEIU's assault on UHW that more tragic and its telling that more crucial. Cal Winslow's groundbreaking account of this epic battle for the soul of trade unionism is indispensible reading for those who believe an injury to one is an injury to all."
— **Sasha Lilley, author of *Capital and Its Discontents***

"The health care workers of California have a terrific tribune in Cal Winslow who has told their bottom-up struggle against the top-down bullying arrogance of the SEIU. Against its might, money, and size the health care workers merely bring solidarity, endurance, and their humble numbers. Moreover, the nurses in standing up for themselves against the Goliath have entered the national health care debate and thus stand up for all. Our health is in their tender, strong hands, so is our labor movement, and our democracy to come. Here is their story! Read it and stand with them shoulder-to-shoulder!"
— **Peter Linebaugh, author of *Magna Carta Manifesto***

"As he provides readers with a front-row seat to the most important struggle inside the union movement, Cal Winslow shows us how union democracy equals worker power, and how rank-and-file volunteers (NUHW) can win against hundreds of so-called "warriors" (paid staff) and the leadership of a corporatist juggernaut called SEIU. Selfless acts of courage by these volunteers inspires solidarity between union and non-union sections of the U.S. working class to fight for democracy within unions and create a more democratic society overall."

— Fernando Gapasin , union activist and labor educator, co-author of *Solidarity Divided: The Crisis in Organized Labor and a New Path Toward Social Justice*

"Cal's writing reminds us what's at stake is larger than our struggle. If unions are truly to be for and about workers, we have to recreate what was lost. Our union improved workers' lives by empowering us to lead the way. Thank you, Cal, for amplifying our voices and for clarifying why our efforts matter."

— Amy Thigpen, M.S.W. Kaiser-Fremont medical social worker and fired steward and treasurer of the Medical Social Work Chapter, SEIU-UHW

"Strange tales from the gothic wing of the capitalist health industry, complete with vampires and leeches. In this instant classic of journalism from below, one of the pioneers of radical social history reports on remarkable signs of life in the morbid body of American labor."

— Iain Boal, historian of the commons

"This little book tells a big story with huge implications—for working people and for democracy. Will the future be handed down from on high, or will it come from the bottom up? In this clear and forthright account of grim developments that have led to the birth of the fledgling NUHW union, Cal Winslow provides the very recent history of a tragic labor debacle that could foreshadow a reinvigorated labor movement from the grassroots. While documenting some morbid events, the message is well-grounded and transcendent: Don't mourn, organize."

— Norman Solomon, author of *War Made Easy: How Presidents and Pundits Keep Spinning Us to Death*

Labor's Civil War in California

The NUHW Healthcare Workers' Rebellion

Cal Winslow

Labor's Civil War in California: The NUHW Healthcare Workers' Rebellion
Cal Winslow
© PM Press 2010 All rights reserved. No part of this book may be transmitted by any
means without permission in writing from the publisher.

ISBN: 978-1-60486-327-7
Library of Congress Control Number: 2010902194

Cover by John Yates
Interior design by briandesign

10 9 8 7 6 5 4 3 2 1

PM Press
PO Box 23912
Oakland, CA 94623
www.pmpress.org

Printed in the USA on recycled paper.

For Samantha

"People find themselves in a society structured in determined ways (crucially, but not exclusively in productive relations), they experience exploitation (or the need to maintain power over those whom the exploit), they identify points of antagonistic interest, they commence to struggle around these issues and in the process of struggling they discover themselves as classes, they come to know this discovery as class consciousness. Class and class consciousness are always the last, not the first, stage in historical development."

— E.P. Thompson, "Eighteenth-Century English Society"

Contents

Introduction

This is the story of a new union, the National Union of Healthcare Workers (NUHW)—a union with great promise, one whose success is of vital importance. It is also, tragically, the story of the destruction of its predecessor, the California local United Healthcare Workers-West (UHW), placed in trusteeship by the Service Employees International Union (SEIU). UHW was widely seen as a "model" union, not just for California labor, but for workers everywhere. It was an outstanding example of union growth and power in an era of trade union stagnation and decline.

The story of this conflict is not always a pleasure to tell. UHW was attacked and wrecked not by the employers and corporate union-busters, not by security guards, not by right-wing vigilantes, and not by the state, but by its own national leadership. Still, it is a story that must be told; for the sake of California's healthcare workers, for those who want to understand this bitter working class war in the West, and because of lessons it can teach us, lessons that will only help us if labor is again to move forward.

This conflict comes at a time when the labor movement in the U.S. private sector is literally engaged in a life-and-death struggle: in 2008, trade union membership in this sector had fallen to 7.6 percent—compared with the high point, 35 percent at the end of World War II. In 2008 there were a mere 15 major (involving 1,000 workers or more) strikes, whereas in 1970 there were nearly 400. Yet UHW grew in this first decade of the new century, more than any other SEIU affiliate; viewed from 2008, it was poised for significant future gains.

This ongoing California conflict, SEIU vs. UHW and now NUHW, is not a local brawl. It is not about personalities, nor about West Coast eccentricities. Its significance is not confined to the fortunes of just one particular union. SEIU's attack, however regrettable, is not the first of its kind—nor will it be the last. We all want the workers united, but the truth is that labor has always been divided, comprised of many currents. The truth is also that there are rights and wrongs in labor, as elsewhere, and that these sometimes expose fundamental divides—in this case, two contesting souls within the workers' movement. These are sharply on display in this dispute: one soul corporatist, authoritarian, top-down, and collaborationist; the other rank-and-file, bottom-up, class-conscious, and combative.

In reality, there exists no sharp, Manichean line dividing the trade union movement down the middle; there are many shades of difference. So, for example, the skilled tradesmen of the end of the nineteenth century, the founders of the American Federation of Labor, were proud elitists, hostile to immigrants and the unskilled, unashamed to be called "business unionists." They persevered, resisting in the 1930s the insurgent industrial unionists. Indeed they are still with us.

Similarly, in the years following World War II, there developed a system of industrial relations based on the rule of the "new men of power" in labor—the leaders of big unions who aspired not just to power at the bargaining table but a place at the table with business, industry and the state.[1] In industrial relations, this new system involved, in labor scholar Kim Moody's terms, "national pattern bargaining, grievance procedures designed to remove conflict from the shop floor, and bureaucratic unionism." It committed workers and their unions to "the body of precedent and methods of functioning" that established this system during the war and "enforced it through the National Labor Relations Board (NLRB), the courts, the industrial wages and benefits pattern and the labor contract" in the years of economic growth following the end of the war.[2] In its own ways, this system worked: permanent labor organizations were established, industry was organized, unions became partners (however junior) in business and industry, and union leaders even (sometimes) advised presidents.

There were alternatives. The AFL was confronted with a national upsurge in class consciousness and radical trade unionism that erupted prior to and during World War I, when, for example, the Industrial Workers of the World (IWW or "Wobblies") raised the banner of "One Big Union" and the specter of revolutionary miners, field hands, and lumberjacks. In these years, the most basic conflicts, often concerning wages, could quickly become movements. Audacious strikes, frequently spontaneous and led by immigrants, were characterized by the use of direct action, working class solidarity, and the demand for industrial unionism.[3]

In the crisis of the early 1930s, the 1934 general strikes in San Francisco, Minneapolis, and Toledo picked up where 1919 left off. The rise of the Congress of Industrial Organizations (CIO), the legalization of trade unions, and the organization of the mass industries were based on the sit-down strike, solidarity, and political action. The war absorbed this movement, anti-communism contained it, and post-war prosperity incorporated it. It was institutionalized in the system described above by Moody, business unionism fitting the era of American hegemony.

One result of the return of economic crisis in the '70s was the collapse, prolonged in this case, of this postwar system in the face of an employers' offensive that began in the late '60s. Trade union leaders, incapable of or unwilling to stand up to employers' demands, were challenged by the rank-and-file rebellions of the "long '70s." These were marked by wildcat strikes, direct action, shop stewards' committees, roving pickets, and confrontations with the authorities, both within the unions and in industry. The demands of the '60s movements—civil rights, women's liberation, participatory democracy—were raised in the trade unions: access, equality, democracy.[4]

Both the AFL and the CIO advanced the labor movement, though in different ways. It was the creation of the CIO that broke the logjam in basic industry. In the '70s, there was advance as well, though this growth was limited to public sector, above all to teachers and public sector workers, where millions joined organized labor. The independent National Education Association (NEA) became the country's single largest labor organization. Manufacturing, however, all but collapsed and blue-collar unionism with it, while in the vast and expanding service sector the unions have yet to win substantial gains.

There were always differences, sometimes fundamental. There was, for example, no love lost between the IWW and the AFL. The latter collaborated with the federal authorizes in the destruction of the Wobblies. The 1930s conflict between the AFL and the CIO was often bloody. In 1969 Jock Yablonski—the dissident miner who opposed the dictatorial rule of United Mine Workers of America (UMWA) leader Tony Boyle—was, for his efforts, shot to death, along with his wife and daughter in their beds on Christmas Eve. The late-'60s conflicts between the Teamsters (IBT) leadership and dissident steel haulers were exceptionally violent. In one incident, the headquarters of the dissidents in Pittsburgh was burned to the ground. The regime of the notorious IBT President Jackie Presser furiously harassed the rank-and-file movement, Teamsters for a Democratic Union (TDU). The first TDU delegate to a national IBT convention was savagely beaten.

These intra-union conflicts fundamentally involved the issue of the willingness of unions and union leaders to stand up to the bosses, but they were often fought out within the unions, when workers demanded their rights not just at work but in their unions, including the right to elect leaders, to freedom of speech, to the approval (or disapproval) of contracts, the right to strike, and so on. While trade unions can be powerful vehicles for workers, they can also be bureaucratic institutions that contain and incorporate working class discontent. It is also the case that the interests of the trade union leaders are not always the same as the interests of the workers. So it seems self-evident that bottom-up, democratic unions are more likely to allow for workers' self-activity, creativity, and their capacity to organize and fight—the prerequisites of winning.

The 2010s are not the 1930s, though this may not be so clear to the unemployed (in Fresno "official" unemployment rose to 15.8 percent in October 2009), never mind those who have lost both their jobs and their homes and must attempt to subsist in the shambles of California's health, welfare and education systems. There are now more than 2.2 million workers in California out of work, more than 12 percent of the workforce.[5] By October 2009 a million and a half California working class families had lost their homes. Surely now, as much as at any time, we need a new labor movement, one that stands up to employers and the state. We need unions that are committed to the organization of all workers, a unionism that speaks to the needs of immigrants, opposes war, and is willing to act—both on behalf of its members and for all workers. That is, we need a movement in the best traditions of the Wobblies and the immigrant workers of the 1910s, the longshoremen of 1934 and the Flint sit-down strikers of 1937 and the rank-and-file rebels of the 1970s. And we don't need a union leadership blocking the path. Samuel Gompers in the 1910s didn't help; neither did William Hutchinson in the '30s, nor George Meany in the '70s. In the case before us, we don't need SEIU President Andy Stern's corporate unionism, and many thousands of California healthcare workers have already said just this.

I should be clear: I support the new NUHW. I believe that the creation of NUHW represents an important step forward for California healthcare workers. This, then, is not an academic exercise. There will be time for that. It is an attempt to tell the story of these California health-care workers—from their point of view. The story needs telling, especially given the superficiality of mainstream media coverage and the reluctance of progressives to offer these workers the support they deserve. At the same time, there are alarms that must be sounded. SEIU is the self-proclaimed vanguard of the American labor movement and there are many who subscribe to this view. Yet SEIU stands exposed in this conflict as never before. Corporate union-ism, Andy Stern's contribution to the retreat of organized labor, can be seen here in stark detail: its backroom deals revealed, its corruption exposed and its dictatorial central-ism and take-no-prisoners style uncovered for all the world to see. Juan Gonzalez, writing in the New York *Daily News*, has posed the problem this way: "After years of claiming the mantle of labor reformer, Stern has shown himself to be an old-fashioned union boss, using snazzy new tactics and rhetoric to achieve absolute control. When will the progres-sive wing of organized labor call him out for what he is?"[6]

I hope this book will help and also that it will draw attention to what is best in labor, represented here by

NUHW. And I want to raise two connected questions. First, which way will take us forward, the path now being charted by NUHW or the corporate unionism of Andy Stern and the SEIU? Which can help give birth to the new labor movement we desperately need? Then, a second question—which side are you on?

The book itself is an independent publication; it is neither sponsored nor financed by NUHW. Members are sure to find errors, misunderstandings, and points of disagreement. I am, of course, solely responsible for the errors. I hope the book will provoke discussion and in so doing clear up misunderstandings and clarify points of agreement and disagreement. We will agree, however, that American workers today face enormous challenges. The point now is that NUHW and its members can, with the support they deserve, play a central role in the movement of healthcare workers, not just in California; indeed they already have. If they are successful at this critical juncture, they can also point the way for others.

I want to acknowledge the support I've been given by NUHW members—workers long accustomed to the fight with the bosses. It has been my great fortune to be associated with them. They now carry a double burden. As so often is the case in this country, workers who demand real change must first of all confront their own union leaders. Today, California healthcare workers face not only hostile management but also what many call the "zombie" SEIU-UHW. In Santa Rosa in late December 2009, workers at Memorial Hospital, culminating a six year campaign, faced down and defeated SEIU. In an open alliance with the management, SEIU-UHW defied the request of the North Bay Labor Council to withdraw from the representational election, ignored the pleas of community and religious leaders, and remained on the ballot solely to strengthen the anti-union vote. Not one single Memorial worker would publicly endorse this "union's" intervention. The result on the union side: NUHW 283 – SEIU-UHW 13.

I also want to call attention to the men and women, the volunteer staff members, who stood by the members, even at the cost of their own jobs. These people—young, not so young, many with families, all dependent on their work for survival—have made an exceptional sacrifice. There is a tradition of sacrifice in the workers' movement, a history of working just for the sake of the struggle. But unfortunately, this tradition has been mostly lost. Not so here: for more than a year now NUHW officers and staff have worked (and they continue to work) as volunteers.[7] They are part of a long and noble tradition.

I want to thank Ramsey Kanaan and PM Press for publishing this book. I would also like to thank Alex Cockburn and Jeffrey St. Clair at *CounterPunch* for providing a platform when few would. Finally, thanks to Steve Early, whose influence is on every page. I am fortunate to have been able to borrow freely from his writings. And thanks, as usual, to Faith Simon.

February 2010, Mendocino County.

CHAPTER ONE

"We Have to Destroy this Union to Save It"

In 2007, national leaders of the Service Employees International Union (SEIU) orchestrated a multi-fronted all-out assault on its powerful, 150,000-member California healthcare workers local union, United Healthcare Workers-West (UHW). The attack was designed to break the union.

SEIU is a large and influential union. It is the nation's second largest union and boasts that it is the fastest-growing union in the United States. Its President, Andy Stern, U. Penn, '71, is perhaps the best-known labor celebrity in the country. He apparently has had more access to the White House than any other individual—22 visits by November 2009.[8] The SEIU is one of the richest unions and spends freely; it reportedly contributed nearly $85 million to the 2008 Obama campaign. The returns for this generosity remain unclear.[9] SEIU's intention in California was to seize control of UHW, remove the elected leaders and relegate its members to other jurisdictions or to altogether new organizations. This goal, formally, was the "trusteeship" of UHW, that is, a hostile take-over, an action that labor journalist Steve Early has described as the trade-union equivalent of "martial law."[10]

SEIU expected resistance, so from the start the attack was all-out, take-no-prisoners. It employed the language of war. In November 2007, top SEIU officials—including Andy Stern and Secretary-Treasurer Anna Burger—held a "War Council," where the plans were developed to dismantle UHW—a "skunk team" was established to discredit UHW and its leaders. The SEIU plan involved, literally, an invasion. It set up a suite of offices, including a "war room" in a "Green Zone" in Oakland.[11] The first skirmish was September 18, 2008, when 70 UHW members overran the chamber, a sign of things to come, chanting, "Whose Union? Our Union!" Speaking at the MGN Grand in Las Vegas, SEIU Executive Vice President Mary Kay Henry referred to the staff preparing the California invasion as "warriors."[12] Bill Ragen, another top staffer, drew, with breathtaking brutality, a parallel with the war in Iraq! "It's like Iraq," Ragen advised SEIU on options, "easy to get in and then a slog"; "implosion might be better," he cautioned in the leaked memo.[13]

"Implosion," Iraq talk, was SEIU headquarters language for breaking UHW up from the inside, in this case carving it up—transferring 65,000 UHW members to a local in Southern California. If trusteeship was pre-emptive, "implosion," in hindsight, seems to have been the long-haul strategy, yet the very fact that it was proposed is an example of the anything-goes mentality that prevails in SEIU. It is also an example of the regard with which SEIU's top leaders holds its members. They showed no interest in the sentiments of these tens of thousands of long-term care workers. This forced transfer still remains on hold, but these options, equally belligerent, were the only ones SEIU considered—no others, no compromise, no mediation (despite offers), no loyal opposition allowed, no "let a hundred flowers bloom!"—instead, a fight to the finish.

In 2007 UHW was SEIU's third largest affiliate. It was then California's second largest SEIU local and the single most powerful labor organization in the state. Taking it down would involve collateral damage: the invasion would necessitate the reorganization virtually of SEIU's entire California operation, which is home to nearly 700,000 SEIU members. New, replacement organizations had to be devised, and most involved separating long-term care workers from hospital workers and others. SEIU spokespeople promoted a statewide local of home-care workers and nursing-home workers as their goal—it still no doubt is. Yet, in every other state where SEIU represents healthcare workers—acute care, nursing home, and home care workers—these workers are all united in a single healthcare workers' union. In California this would mean 350,000 workers in one local. There were other designs, and some no doubt remain in the imaginations of the union's ever plotting central staff. But no elections were projected. Once in place, the majority of SEIU members in California would be in "trusteed" locals, as indeed they are now. These schemes had this in common: whatever the outcome, the California SEIU would be managed directly from the SEIU national headquarters in Washington, D.C., through appointed surrogates.

The SEIU campaign combined organizational, political, and legal attacks. These included formal legal charges against leaders, the dismantling of workplace organizations and the replacement of elected union officers right down to the stewards. It thrived on the harassment of individual members. The first phase lasted a year; indeed, it continues, a relentless onslaught against NUHW and its members including the destruction of the workers' base, workplace organizations that were the result of decades of struggle. Particularly vicious has been the legal assault—specious lawsuits conceived by highly compensated attorneys to bankrupt and humiliate former UHW staff.

SEIU sent many hundreds of staff into California, and spent many millions of dollars. The savagery of the assault was bewildering to insiders and outsiders alike. For most of the former UHW staff and members, it has been a long, ongoing nightmare, a conflict imposed with no reasonable justification whatsoever. It is endured only because of the righteousness of the cause. Protests were widespread, including from labor councils throughout California.[14] Mike Casey, the leader of San Francisco's Central Labor Council and President of UNITE HERE Local 2, opposed the intervention from the beginning. "I believe that there must always be room within organized labor for legitimate and principled dissent," he said. "The public discourse initiated by UHW and Sal Rosselli may well be kicking up a lot of dust, but it has also provoked a closer examination of the direction of our movement."[15]

Wrecking UHW would be no cake-walk; not even SEIU predicted dancing in the streets. The local's 150,000 members made it larger than many national unions. It had 100 elected executive board members, 85 of whom were working members. These workers are overwhelmingly people of color, mostly women, often immigrants—UHW members spoke more than 50 languages. UHW had deep roots, in particular in Northern California, where it began in 1938, the first hospital union in the country. It was born in the aftermath of the San Francisco General Strike, when longshoremen led an historic rank-and-file rebellion, inspiring the transformation of industrial relations on the Pacific Coast. Hospital porters led the drive to organize San Francisco General Hospital—from the bottom up.

In 2008 UHW members in its hospital division had the highest standards in the industry in the nation: wages, fully-paid health, defined pension plans, a real voice in hospital staffing and patient care, as well as employment and income security. This in an industry dominated by fiercely anti-union corporations. UHW's contracts with Kaiser Permanente were referred to as the "gold standard," the best acute-care agreements in the U.S. It was a fighting union. UHW was the single fastest growing local union in SEIU. Since 2000 it had organized nearly 75,000 workers, doubling its size in eight years. The power of this union was seen in the 60-day strike in 2005 against Sutter Health's California Pacific Medical Center, one of the most profitable hospitals in the country. The strike issues were organizing rights for the unorganized and the right of caregivers to have a voice in how the hospital would be staffed. UHW's new members accounted for almost all of SEIU's growth in hospitals.

UHW was democratic, certainly by trade-union standards. There were elections at every single level. Its structure was egalitarian—from its universal system of elected shop stewards, stewards' councils, and divisional bodies to its elected executive committee. UHW prided itself on workplace organization and member involvement. Interestingly, in January 2009, just days before trusteeship was imposed, Rosselli and the other officers were reelected—overwhelmingly in a thoroughly fair election—in spite of the international's year-long "skunk" campaign of defamation and disinformation. Under trusteeship there will be no elections.

Rosselli is a former nursing home worker who won an insurgent campaign in the 1988s, challenging an SEIU leadership slate in the aftermath of a trusteeship. He went on to lead what was then Local 250, rebuilding the union by emphasizing democratic decision making and worker militancy. Then, as now, Kaiser was the center of power in the union. UHW was also a progressive union; it opposed war and supported social justice. Its support for universal healthcare dated back to the 1980s, when it supported Proposition 186, the single-payer healthcare initiative. It was a founding member of U.S. Labor Against the War (USLAW) in Iraq. It helped UNITE-HERE members win their "two-year war"—a strike and lock-out that rocked the

San Francisco hotel industry in 2004–2006. Among other things, UHW persuaded Kaiser to maintain hotel strikers' healthcare benefits. UHW led, with the California teachers, the trade union fight against Proposition 8, the anti-same-sex marriage referendum narrowly passed in November 2008. Rosselli is a past Grand Marshall of San Francisco's annual Gay Pride Parade.

Why wreck this union? Why exactly SEIU chose this course of action remains a question to this day: hubris, retaliation, a rapacious, sectarian organizational perspective? All of the above? How can we know for sure? What possibly could justify an intervention on this scale?

There were no murders, no dissenters shot. There were no beatings, no mobsters, no fleets of Cadillacs, no double or triple salaries, no lavish accommodations, nothing like SEIU's Gus Bevona's marble-and-mahogany palace in New York City in the 1990s. As labor historian Nelson Lichtenstein testified before the trusteeship hearing officer,

> In this instance, from what I know ... it strikes me
> as a local in which there is no self-serving, self-
> interested strata of leaders who seek to perpetuate
> their leadership for criminal or self-aggrandizing
> purposes. Instead it is a democratic, open union—
> in some ways a model union. I wish there were more
> like United Healthcare West.[16]

SEIU's formal complaints came in a March 24, 2008, letter from Stern to Rosselli, with copies to the UHW Executive Board. The letter consisted of a list of charges: 1) that UHW leaders had created a "shadow entity," namely the healthcare education fund; 2) that UHW "undermined" negotiations with five California nursing home chains; 3) that the local conducted "a deceptive and phony mail ballot" concerning the union preferences of long-term care workers; 4) that it "colluded" with the California Nurses Association (CNA);

5) that it developed a plan to "destabilize and decertify" bargaining units within SEIU; 6) that it employed a range of tactics that were "chilling membership free-speech rights"; and 7) and that it colluded to undermine SEIU affiliation talks for teachers in Puerto Rico.[17]

I don't believe anyone really took these charges seriously. Within the year Stern would announce his own sleazy deal with the CNA. As for "collusion" regarding the Puerto Rican teachers, laughable. Undermining bargaining? UHW had the best healthcare contracts in the country; it was in negotiations representing nearly 80,000 workers. "Chilling" members' voices—please.

There were, however, two issues of substance. First, the charge that UHW was guilty of "financial malfeasance" struck a chord with some, and in the end this was the charge that became the basis of its case for trusteeship. In 2007, UHW set up a healthcare education trust fund—some $6 million was to be set aside for the purpose of campaigning on healthcare issues. News of this fund set off alarms in the inner chambers of SEIU. It reacted by charging UHW with essentially setting up a self-defense fund, the basis, it suspected, of a possible union within the union, "a shadow entity." This, of course, was strongly contested by UHW, which nonetheless responded by disbanding the fund. SEIU took UHW to court but could not find a compliant judge. Instead, a district court judge dismissed all charges, finding nothing amiss and declaring SEIU's solicitations to be without merit. Ray Marshall, the trusteeship hearing officer, would find this charge insufficient to justify trusteeship.[18]

Second, SEIU charged that UHW was obstructing the forced transfer of 65,000 long-term care workers to Tyrone Freeman's Local 6434 in Southern California. This charge was, strictly speaking, true but was a bit more complicated. On the surface it was a simple organizational issue—but why was SEIU pressing such fundamental jurisdictional realignments in California? And why should UHW willingly accept this industrial partition that would mean the loss of nearly half its membership, without debate or the consent of the members involved? Yet at SEIU's 2008 San Juan convention, Stern had rammed through a "jurisdictional change," paving the way for the home care and nursing home employees to be moved from UHW to Freeman's local.

But much more was involved—and both sides knew it. Beneath this jurisdictional controversy there were foundational issues at stake that went right to the heart of the trade union project.

The place to begin is the San Juan convention, where the dispute was framed theoretically. The international explained the alleged transgressions of UHW as symptoms of deeper villainies. *Justice for All*, the document of the majority in San Juan, laid out the perspectives of the leadership, justifying, among other things, the transfer of the 65,000. These included, implicitly, a condemnation of UHW, its practice and its leadership. In San Juan UHW opposed the international leadership's perspectives, the only healthcare local union to do so. That, in turn brought further charges: UHW—unwilling to abandon its own views and the results of decades of building—was charged with, in effect, defying national perspectives, that is, of defying the will of the majority. No small matter, in SEIU's conception of the importance of "democratic" centralism.

Stephen Lerner, an SEIU leader, however, alleged that UHW was guilty of far more than the misdemeanors, real or imagined, listed above. According to Lerner, who was once celebrated as architect of the 1990 Justice for Janitors campaign, UHW "had reverted to a 1950s strategy of dedicating the union's resources to existing members instead of building a broader workers movement." UHW, with its "just us" strategy (SEIU's label for the UHW document *Platform for Change*[19]) did this, according to Lerner; it focused "the

union on servicing and defending remaining islands of
unionization (i.e. local union interest)." He called this
"neo-business unionism," adding that it was "a prescription of death for the labor movement."[20] So there we have
it—pretty serious! UHW, according to SEIU, advanced "a
prescription of death for the labor movement!"

"Neo-business unionism" is a new species, yet to be
fleshed out, but its elaboration might well merit a generous
SEIU grant. Still to give SEIU its due: *Justice for All*, Lerner
said,

> is both an ideological and practical commitment to
> build a movement for all workers to win broad goals
> to change and transform the country: healthcare for
> all, immigration reform, quality public services for
> our communities, and the organization of millions
> of workers in the South and other non-union regions
> of the country. Combined with a commitment to
> work to build a global labor movement and a focus
> on getting out of Iraq, the program adopted by
> SEIU delegates is one of the most progressive and
> ambitious of a major union in recent history. The
> most radical development from the SEIU Convention
> is that delegates overwhelmingly voted to commit
> SEIU to changing the world.[21]

Strong words. We'd all like to change the world. But I hope
we can be forgiven for taking Lerner with a grain of salt. It
seems quite plain here that he was simply raising the stakes
(rhetorically) as high as possible, thus making reconciliation even theoretically impossible.

According to SEIU spokesman Andy McDonald, UHW
was also in violation of Stern's "one voice," "one national
strategy" rule.[22] "The issue," he said, "is that there's a disagreement about the fact that there are democratic decision-making procedures in SEIU," a reference to the SEIU

one-party system and a cliché which has an all too familiar sectarian ring, the classic justification for a purge.[23] Minorities are fine as long as they loyally toe the line and go away between conventions.

John Borsos, the UHW administrative vice president, responded for the local union: "There *was* consensus within SEIU that the labor movement is in crisis," he stated.

> In broad strokes, there is consensus that they way out of this crisis is by organizing the unorganized, building political power, and holding elected officials accountable, and improving standards through coordinated regional, national, and international bargaining that enhances the lives of workers, their families, and those who rely on their services. These goals should be the bread and butter for all self-respecting trade unionists. Who could possibly be against them?[24]

"The dispute," he argued, was

> about how we accomplish these goals and what kind of labor movement we are building in the process. To put it simply, will the labor movement be a movement of workers, by workers, and for workers, driven from the bottom up? Or will it be a centralized, top-down advocacy organization where workers pay membership fees in exchange for professional services?[25]

CHAPTER TWO

"The Boss Brought Us This Union"

There are more than a thousand skilled nursing facilities (nursing homes) in California. Tens of thousands work in these "homes," which John Borsos has called "the sweat-shops of the twenty-first century. The hours are long, the pay low, and the work heavy and dangerous. Sal Rosselli, in a 2005 interview, assessed the state of UHW members this way:

> Some of our members make a fair and decent living, but not most of them. It's taken us decades to win fair wages and benefits and approaching a fair pension with Kaiser Permanente. That's probably our best single contract. In the nursing home industry, it's not true at all. Our nursing home members have to work two jobs to make things meet. We have a long way to go with long-term care workers and a long way to go with unorganized hospital workers.[26]

Andy Stern noted in 2007 that "Ninety percent of nursing home workers in this country live pretty much in poverty. Don't have unions, don't have healthcare. All of our activities to date to solve that part of the problem have not worked."[27]

What to do about this? What is a platform for "justice," including for California long-term care workers? As clearly as anywhere, we can understand this conflict in terms of the systems of industrial relations that prevail, certainly in the absence of unions, in California's healthcare industry— systems that produce poverty, healthcare workers without healthcare, workers who need to work two jobs because one won't do, not to mention the barriers to decent conditions and decent lives for those who live in these homes.

Consider this example. SEIU, in 2003, promoted the idea of an "Alliance" of nursing home employers and their employees, organized or to be organized by SEIU. At the center of this organizing "experiment" was "neutrality." That is, an agreement on the part of the employers not to oppose, within highly specific parameters, union organizing. SEIU, of course, is not alone in attempting to win employer "neutrality" in organizational campaigns; the now-stalled Employee Free Choice Act (EFCA) is, in essence, based on this.

The problem is that collective bargaining in the United States is increasingly rare. The great majority of workers (88 percent) face employers of whatever size, from Wal-Mart to the corner store, on their own. Today, moreover, the new contract is as likely to bring concessions as improvements—a pattern established in the '80s that continues to this day and is often evident in the rollback of healthcare benefits. The unions have been losing. Still all accounts reveal that it is better to have a union than no union—wages, benefits, quality of work life, etc. And no wonder. The new year's economic reports inform us that the past decade was one of the worst for workers in U.S. history. There was zero job creation in the years since 1999, and working class Americans earn less, when wages are adjusted for inflation, than they did in 1999.[28]

The basic idea, then, is that if workers are to begin to win, they need a "free choice" in choosing whether or not to have a union—that is, a choice free from employer interference and intimidation. It is incontestable that stubborn employer opposition underlies trade union decline. Thus the significance of the victory in SEIU's 1990 Justice for Janitors strike that resulted, in part, from the union's achievement of a neutrality pact with employers.

The "Alliance" strategy, developed for California nursing homes, was in line with SEIU fundamentals: first in that trade-union density in targeted industries (long-term care in this case) was the precondition for real progress; and second that in today's conditions "new" methods of organizing—partnerships—were essential.[29] At the time, the "Alliance" employers represented 284 homes, about a quarter of the homes in California. SEIU, bargaining with these employers, agreed to mount a campaign in Sacramento to win "rate reform," that is increased funding for nursing homes from Medi-Cal, the California Medicaid program. In return, the nursing home employers gave the union the right to organize 42 homes, which they selected. According a UHW review of the Alliance agreement, made public in early 2007,

> Members had little say in reaping the benefits of that agreement. The collective bargaining agreement for newly organized Alliance workers (the template) had little, if any, member involvement, nor did having a say on the amount of money that ultimately became the 'economic deal' in negotiations for wages and benefits. In short, the template and the economic deal were cut at the top. It became part of the business transaction with the nursing home employers.[30]

There are, it is plain to see, multiple problems here. The union, to its credit, was successful in pressuring Sacramento to increase funding to nursing homes, a needed reform, although also a bonanza for the employers. However, aside from the right to organize 42 homes, what did the union achieve for its members? UHW projected that by the end of 2007 while the Alliance homes would receive nearly $120 million in new revenues, the employers would spend only about $20 million on improvements to SEIU members' contracts. Moreover, if the template was re-negotiated, the union's organizing would again be restricted to a limited number of homes, selected by the employers—this when the entire industry was benefiting by hundreds of millions. On the issue of density (the number of members in an industry or region), according to the report, even if the Alliance employers were to allow 100 percent density in their sphere—highly unlikely—that would leave the remaining 75 percent of the nursing home industry in California non-union, effectively off-limits for SEIU.

And what about the workers? The contract that the newly organized workers received was worked out on high in advance with the ultimate terms of that agreement discouraging, and in some cases preventing, workers from independently engaging in struggle to improve their working conditions. The UHW report concluded that from "member's experience it is safe to state that the template arrangement created a worker organization that restricts member empowerment." And it is no wonder many workers quite rightly complained that "the boss brought us this union."[31]

The restrictions? The agreement obliged the union to press for tort reform that would limit patients' right to sue in cases of neglect, abuse, or even death. It obliged the union to oppose patient advocates demands for staffing minimums and any legislation related to the nursing homes industry, without industry approval. An example: "the SEIU will oppose any long-term-care-specific staffing and reimbursement legislation or regulation that fails to meet mutually agreed objectives." (At the time a UHW survey of 1,600 members under Alliance contracts revealed that short staffing, and how it compromises their ability to provide quality care for residents, was the number one complaint.)

In addition, SEIU agreed to give employers control over which facilities could be organized. It banned strikes and limited collective bargaining and prohibited organizing, even where workers wanted to organize—unless the industry agreed. The agreement gave employers "exclusive rights to manage the business"—that is the standard management's rights clause, power over the entire work process ("employers have the exclusive right to manage the business"). It agreed that the union would not demand pay rates or benefits that put employer at an economic disadvantage.

The trading away of workers' rights to free speech is particularly problematic, however desperate economic circumstances may be—problematic not just for the caregivers but for patients, families and advocates of nursing home reform. The SEIU, in agreeing to restrict members from reporting poor nursing home conditions to state regulators, made a concession and gave up a basic right few could support. One advocate explained it this way: "This is a sector where caregivers are the eyes and ears and the witnesses when there is abuse. To tie their hands and to tie their tongues is to let people die. That's immoral and a terrible thing for a nursing home worker to have to live with."[32]

In These Times reporter David Moberg observed that employer "neutrality" is at best contradictory. The difficulty in winning leads unions to substitute external campaigns for worker organizing. The result is often, as with the Nursing Home Alliance, "that they deny workers a fully functioning union."[33] To say the least! (Skeptics need only review an alliance agreement still in force in Washington State.) In the California Alliance agreement, SEIU gave nursing home workers an agreement in which workers lost more than they gained.

In 2007, the Alliance came up for renewal. SEIU wanted to renew the agreement—now as a "template," that is, a pattern for all such agreements, no longer to be an experiment. The employers proposed, among other things, the old restrictions plus new ones, a 50-year agreement, which was then "revised" to 20 years.[34] Both the International Union and Local 6434, (the new Southern California long-term care local created in a series of mergers and led then by Tyrone Freeman) supported such an agreement.

This was unacceptable to UHW, which at that time represented 80 percent of the Alliance's organized workers. Renewing the agreement, the local claimed, would "adversely affect our mission and goal to advance and defend the interests of our members and in fact may come close to becoming what have historically been called 'company unions.'"[35] Thousands of UHW members petitioned to end it. The SEIU response, typically, schemes and maneuvers. First it proposed an election in which just three parties would vote—UHW, Local 6434, and the International—with one vote each. Then it met separately with the Alliance employers and predictably began its campaign against Rosselli and the leaders of UHW. Opposition to renewal of the Alliance agreement, with strong support from consumer advocates and residents, scuttled it—at least in California. Nevertheless, Stern continues to support the template. With his next move, Stern retaliated, first with the threat of trusteeship and then the proposed removal of all UHW long-term care workers into 6434—now the largest local in the state, home of 120,000 long-term care workers, and the lowest paid in the state.

The *sine qua non* of SEIU—certainly since the 2005 creation of Change to Win (CtW)—has been, above all else, growth. CtW, now in shambles, is the federation of national unions that left the AFL-CIO that year. Organized labor, according to SEIU, must grow, and grow rapidly. Only density can carry the unions to the next industry and the next region. Only increasing density can guarantee labor a future. Possibly. And fair enough, given the state of organized labor. But the SEIU then proposes what amounts, abstractly, to an all-or-nothing and highly sectarian strategy of organizing, in effect substituting itself for the entire labor movement if not the working class. All alternatives strategies are doomed to failure, if not reactionary. Partial victories are unacceptable, Lerner writes, the "scale is always too small."[36]

A recent report from UNITE HERE, still a partner of SEIU's in CtW, helps us put this argument in perspective. The UNITE HERE analysis reveals that SEIU remains, all boasting aside, a small union in a vast, complex and little-understood working class. The National Education Association, the teachers' union, is the largest union by more than a million members and justifiably can speak of density. SEIU, on the contrary, represents at best 10 percent of the hospital workers in the United States, and perhaps 10–12 percent of nursing home workers. SEIU's hospital workers are concentrated in a handful of states, especially in the mega-locals 1199/United Healthcare East and SEIU-UHW. The largest concentration is the New York Metropolitan area, then the San Francisco Bay Area, Sacramento, and Los Angeles. The latter three represent, of course, the work of the now-wrecked UFW. Seattle is fifth. According to the UNITE HERE report, "The relatively low level of union density in hospitals, and the heavy concentration of SEIU's membership on the coasts, leaves the union with minimal density in large swaths of the country, even in markets where one would expect a strong SEIU hospital presence." The report suggests that 1199 West Virginia/Kentucky/Ohio ("old boy Dave Regan's" onetime stomping ground), "after years of organizing," has miniscule density in its tri-state jurisdiction: 1.7 percent. It finds the similar results in Illinois and Indiana: "the recently formed SEIU Healthcare Illinois & Indiana claims to be 'the voice of more than seven thousand health systems and social service workers.'" Yet there are 299,113 eligible hospital workers in Illinois and Indiana, meaning that in these two large states, the maximum possible SEIU density is 2.3 percent.[37]

And if SEIU's "density" is less than claimed, what about its overall strength? SEIU boasts "record-setting growth" since President Andy Stern took office in 1996. Since then, according to SEIU, it has grown by more than one million members, increasing the union's membership to nearly 2 million overall, surely an accomplishment and a contrast with mainstream unions. But critics are skeptical.[38] The case now in point is Stern's attempt to absorb tens of thousands of UNITE HERE members in a raid that has united much of labor against him. "The SEIU under Stern,'" writes Juan Gonzalez, "is fast becoming the Roman Empire of the Labor movement ... Stern is forever on the prowl for new workers to absorb into his empire and he doesn't much care how he does it..."[39] The largest single group of new members is comprised of long-term care workers—more than 500,000. But while this achievement is a step forward, it is important to understand that these workers, until recently treated as independent contractors, have been organized *en masse*, often as the result of deals with state governors and local politicians. The 1998 merger with New York's Local 1199 brought in another 200,000. At the same time there is no evidence that CtW has grown at all. As for global organizing, if the raid on the Puerto Rican teachers' union is an example of "growth" then the metaphor of empire is all too apt—and far from an adventure to be acclaimed; rather this SEIU "globalism," hardly a reminder that the workers have no country, is just another grim reminder of the depth of the imperial prospect in this society.

One more point about partnerships. Was the "Alliance an exception? A mistake? Not for SEIU. Concurrently with the Alliance debacle, SEIU negotiated agreements with Sodexho, Compass, and Aramark—large corporations that subcontract work for hospitals, schools, and industry. In these cases the international union staff conducted negotiations, gaining employer neutrality in a number of areas. Flabbergasted, many local officers and SEIU members reported they were unaware that such deals even existed, let alone their details.[40]

In 2006 and 2007, California SEIU locals, led by UHW, were negotiating a new contract with Tenet, the then scandal-ridden chain with a dozen hospitals in California and many more strung across the South—the nation's second largest for-profit hospital system. The renewal followed an initial 2003 agreement in which Tenet agreed to stay neutral when workers sought to organize in California and three hospitals in Florida. For more than a year in advance of the bargaining, rank-and-file leaders from each SEIU-represented hospital in Florida and California organized a Tenet Unity Council to establish bargaining goals, a committee including nearly 100 union rank-and-file leaders, workers elected to the bargaining by thousands of their co-workers—a standard procedure in UHW bargaining.

Bargaining goals included winning industry-standard contracts in Florida and California and winning organizing rights for workers in the rest of the Tenet system. Before bargaining commenced in September 2006, Tenet expressed concern about the financial impacts of the California bargaining, while at the same time indicating a willingness to extend organizing rights outside California. But Tenet demanded relief from union standards in California in exchange for extending these rights.

Initially, Tenet made two demands as preconditions for extending organizing rights: that the unions agree not to pursue either a defined benefit pension plan or retiree healthcare coverage in this round of bargaining. In response, SEIU members collectively established their own preconditions: that with the exception of pension and retiree health, Tenet would have to agree to all other standards—including staffing language, a ban on subcontracting, wage scales, and other significant improvements—in addition to extending organizing rights to workers outside California.

Then, when it came to actually negotiating the contract, this collective was abandoned and SEIU staff commandeered negotiations, focusing instead on the only part of the agreement they cared about: organizing rights outside California. In December 2006, SEIU announced they had reached a tentative agreement with Tenet for organizing rights for 23 hospitals throughout the United States. What had they given up? SEIU representatives agreed to give up workers' right to strike in California for ten years, to allow the company to subcontract up to 12 percent of the workforce at any time, and to give away job security provisions already contained in the contract.

Aware of the massive rank-and-file opposition to the agreement, SEIU as usual devised an electoral scheme. The Unity Council, elected on a per-capita basis, was dominated by UHW members. So the International—then through its healthcare division steering committee headed by Dennis Rivera, the well-known leader of New York City's healthcare workers—proposed that this steering committee make all final decisions. As this too proved unacceptable, Judy Scott, an SEIU attorney, proposed the following (really): there were 9,000 organized workers in Tenet, the majority members of UHW. But there were 12,000 unorganized workers. Shouldn't they too have a voice, Scott argued? SEIU responded that they should, and, with all its usual generosity, agreed to vote by proxy on their behalf.

Michael Torres, a respiratory therapist at U.S.C. University Hospital in Los Angeles, then part of the Tenet Healthcare Corporation, said, "Stern's approach had hurt Tenet employees." He complained that "the union leaders had sought to make a deal that called for not pushing for pensions or retiree health coverage; in exchange Tenet would not fight unionization of eleven facilities in Florida.

"We were handicapped from the get-go in our negotiations," Torres said. "We were fighting not only the employer but the international union. I think we need a major correction within the union if we are going to build a sustainable organization." [41]

In the end, Tenet, faced with the opposition of thousands of mobilized UHW members in California, withdrew its concessionary demands. The California workers had sacrificed to win organizing rights outside of California, and settled for contract standards below the state's norms—at Kaiser Permanente, Catholic Healthcare West, the Daughters of Charity Health System, and HCA. But the experience for healthcare workers was that the oft-heralded power of SEIU seemed to be used in the interests of the industry as often as in their own. [42]

According to Rosselli, "We have always had relations with employers, but we have approached even cooperation from a standpoint of strength. We can't surrender traditional rights, like the right to picket, to strike or to bargain ... [The problem] is the drive for growth at all costs, without taking into account standards that need to be raised at the same time." [43]

Stephen Lerner calls this "I've-got-mine" unionism, "servicing existing members," as if the nursing home worker demanding a raise is shortsighted and selfish. [44] It is difficult to understand a perspective that belittles the struggle for immediate gains, all the more so in current conditions. More, there is no reason to suspect that gains won here today might not inspire demands elsewhere tomorrow. Isn't struggle infectious? Workers can have what they want; it just depends on how well organized they are and how hard they fight.

SEIU apparently does not believe this. The idea of struggle, the class struggle, Stern tells us, represents "a mentality that was a vestige of an earlier, rough era of industrial unionism." [45] In its place, SEIU offers delayed gratification. But this is the viewpoint of the employers—it is sacrifice now, accept cutbacks, make concessions, save up your grievances. Your reward will be in the future, you can count on us! "You'll get pie in the sky when you die!" sang the Wobblies.

CHAPTER THREE

"A Very Troubling Message"

The SEIU-UHW dispute became public in April 2007, when *SF Weekly* writer Matt Smith disclosed the contents of leaked SEIU contracts, memos, and reports related to the Alliance issues, including the UHW document, *The California Alliance Agreement*. Smith, not always the favorite of UHW leaders, took apart the 2003 nursing home agreement and concluded: "This is the new era of worker-employer collaboration touted in Stern's book, and in articles that characterize him as a bold 'modernizer.'" Journalists, he continued, had failed to find out just "what exactly [Stern] was talking about." If they had, they would have discovered a "monumental catch"—the workers who joined the SEIU as part of the 2003 agreement, an agreement that is supposed to be a national model for corporate collaboration, "get a severely stripped-down version of union representation."[46]

Stern was furious; a campaign of character assassination was unleashed, one aimed not just at Rosselli. The UHW was charged with, among other things, opposition to "employer agreements" and concern only about "polishing the apple" for its own members, not about organizing workers outside California. Rosselli, responding directly to Stern, denied UHW responsibility for the leaked documents: "The UHW analysis of the California Alliance was produced at your request in January and was widely distributed throughout the Long Term Care Division and SEIU." Concerning "polishing the apple," Rosselli answered,

> We do not believe, nor are we willing to tell Kaiser Permanente members, that they should be satisfied with the wages and benefits we have collectively achieved. Our Kaiser Permanente members seek higher standards for their families and patients and still continue to pool their dues dollars to improve their standards as well as the standards of other healthcare workers.

Rosselli also expressed concern about the "lack of a safe environment within SEIU to voice disagreement." "We've seen quite clearly" in the fallout from the *SF Weekly* article, "that it is not acceptable for leaders to disagree. Disagreement is equated with disloyalty." [47]

In late 2007 Rosselli stepped down as head of the SEIU State Council, in part the result of his opposition to Stern's healthcare deal with California Governor Arnold Schwarzenegger.[48] The following February he resigned from the SEIU's International Executive Committee, citing conflicts with the majority on issues including membership rights, union democracy, corruption and the SEIU's "alliance" strategy—its "low road" approach to settling with nursing home managements.[49]

On March 27, 2008, the public learned of the proposed trusteeship in a *San Francisco Chronicle* feature that reported that Stern "moved this week to oust the leaders of its West Coast affiliate" alleging "misconduct" by Rosselli and others. Rosselli's retort, reported the *Chronicle*: "It's retaliatory because we are speaking out against his ideology, his direction. The simplest way I can say it is, it's top-down versus bottom-up, corporate unionism versus social unionism." [50]

News of the SEIU's planned trusteeship caused disquiet in labor and progressive circles, especially in California where UHW had widespread connections and strong allies, especially on San Francisco's powerful Central Labor Council. Outside California, reaction was more subdued and the "we can't get involved in internal union affairs" mantra seemed to rule. This was not helped, however, by SEIU's April antics in Michigan. The union sent busloads of members from Ohio to the *Labor Notes* conference in Dearborn to confront leaders and members of the California Nurses Association (CNA), as well as a large delegation of UHW members. SEIU, then in a jurisdictional dispute with CNA, considered nurses "union busters."

New York Times labor reporter Stephen Greenhouse reported that fighting began when service employee members and officials tried to barge into the conference in a hotel banquet hall.[51] The attack—organized by now-disgraced former California SEIU leader Rickman Jackson and assisted by, yes, "old school," now trustee Dave Regan—might have been merely comical had not a retired member of the United Automobile Workers been pushed. She banged her head against a table and was taken to a hospital for a head wound. Worse, one of the rent-a-mob, home care worker David Smith, collapsed as the result of a heart attack and died in the aftermath of the melee. This would not be the last such assault.

AFL-CIO President John Sweeney denounced what he called "a violent attack orchestrated" by SEIU against members of other unions. There is no justification, none, for the violent attack orchestrated by SEIU."[52]

More than 100 academics, labor educators, and intellectuals, including many who identified themselves as long-time friends of SEIU, voiced concerns about the trusteeship threat in a May Day open letter to Andy Stern. Noam Chomsky, Howard Zinn, Adolph Reed, Elaine Bernard,

Vijay Prashad, Eileen Boris, Jennifer Klein, Marcus Rediker, and Mike Davis were among the signers who warned that "putting UHW under trusteeship would send a very troubling message and be viewed, by many, as a sign that internal democracy is not valued or tolerated within SEIU." It was published in the *New York Times*.[53]

Stern responded to the scholars: "SEIU values the ideas, opinions, and views of the many people who work with labor from the progressive community."[54] He insisted that "debate, dissent, and new ideas are encouraged" within his union. In fact, he found it "puzzling" that UHW could possibly think that "its opinions are not welcome and could lead to trusteeship." Eliseo Medina and Gerry Hudson, well-known SEIU vice presidents, chastised the concerned labor educators; "the only talk of trusteeship has come from [UHW] itself."[55] As late as mid-July 2008, SEIU spokesman Lerner scoffed at the "myth that UHW has been threatened with trusteeship." He reassured readers that "this simply isn't true, no matter how often repeated" and claimed that such "misinformation" and "left rhetoric about militant struggle, better contracts ... and greater local autonomy" were just a "distraction" from the "vibrant, open honest debate" that needs to go on about how labor can secure what he calls *Justice for All*. But for Lerner, UHW was standing in the way, with its "'Left Business Unionism,' or maybe more appropriately, 'Neo-Business Unionism.'"[56]

Stern himself suggested to the May Day signers that UHW might be simply confusing "rebuttal and robust debate with retaliation."[57] So much for telling the truth to your friends.

Reading Stern's response, even academics who were initially skeptical about the likelihood of influencing SEIU behavior began to express optimism. This is one "pre-emptive strike that might work," declared Stanley Aronowitz, a labor scholar at the City University of New

York (CUNY). "Stern has already responded and waffles on the trusteeship issue, but is quite defensive. Yet his tone is moderate and looks forward to further 'dialogue' with the signers."[58]

Dan Clawson, a sociologist at the University of Massachusetts Amherst, read the Stern letter as "serious and engaged." He expressed the hope that there might actually be some "much-needed dialogue."[59] All too true—but this was not to be. To this day, I know of not one single example of SEIU leaders engaging in public discussion or debate on this subject. On the contrary they have rejected all invitations, boycotted all meetings, and "encouraged" their supporters to do the same. In November 2009 they reverted to their *Labor Notes* tactics and blockaded a San Francisco NUHW fundraiser with hundreds of staff and bused in "lost timers," SEIU members paid for performing this task. The fundraiser was to assist individual former UHW leaders who collectively face hundreds of thousands of dollars in legal fees—the result of ongoing SEIU legal harassment. The next night they attacked a public meeting at the offices of the United Teachers of Los Angeles, blocking entrances and throwing eggs and bottles at those attending.[60]

Public discussion, dialogue, and debate—even internal debate—are not the SEIU style. "In the SEIU," writes Herman Benson, director of the Association for Union Democracy, "Andy Stern would have the whole union leadership, top to bottom, local and international, elective and appointive, acting as one monolithic bloc, speaking to the membership with one united voice in favor of the official line."[61]

Nevertheless, and for reasons still unknown, SEIU then retreated on trusteeship—but only to throw down a new gauntlet. "Implosion" now came front and center, partly as a serious option, but also as a tactic in its ongoing effort to disrupt, disunite and discourage UHW and its members—more mailers, robo-calls, accusations. UHW was informed that 65,000 home care workers—nearly half the UHW membership—were to be removed involuntarily and reassigned to Tyrone Freeman's Los Angeles-based Local 6434. SEIU, it seemed, might have to tolerate the UHW dissidents for a while longer, but only in a much smaller local.

Freeman's rise to prominence in SEIU was spectacular, but probably not altogether unique. He came to California in 1999 from Atlanta where he first became an SEIU full-timer. In 2006, as part of a reorganization dictated from headquarters, he was appointed president of the giant new Local 6434. Freeman was also appointed president of California United Homecare Workers—a joint venture between SEIU and the American Federation of State, County and Municipal Employees (AFSCME)—altogether he "led" nearly 200,000 California long-term care workers and was paid more than $200,000 a year for it. In SEIU, he joined the international Executive Committee in 1996, the youngest person to do so in the union's history. In 2000 he became a vice president of the international.

Few UHW long-term care union were fans of Freeman. He was viewed as a weak negotiator, less aggressive than Rosselli in upholding SEIU contract standards. In balloting conducted by UHW in 2008, the affected members voted by a large margin to stay in UHW. But what the members wanted did not matter in Washington. Stern organized a two-day "jurisdictional hearing," held in mid-July in Manhattan Beach, California. There more than 5,000 UHW members laid siege to the hotel where the hearing was held. They protested any decision by the Stern-appointed hearing officer that would tear their local apart and, according to UHW supporters, "doom healthcare workers in California to years of substandard contracts and a weakened voice in patient care." [62]

Internal foes of dismemberment were backed by outsiders who shared that concern. Both feared that Stern wanted to revive the industry-wide "Alliance" deal with nursing home operators that compromised SEIU's ability to engage in patient advocacy and make a deal that failed to deliver promised improvements in pay, benefits, and workloads for union members. In an open letter dated July 9, 2008, UC-San Francisco sociologist and nursing professor Charlene Harrington, a researcher on nursing home financing, applauded a different kind of contract, recently negotiated by UHW with Mariner Health Care facilities in Northern California. That agreement, she contended, "empowers caregivers to stand up for their residents" and "shows there is a better path to improve nursing home quality." According to Harrington, SEIU's attempt to push UHW out of long-term care lobbying and bargaining "may have serious negative consequences for nursing home residents and quality care." [63]

But it was Freeman, a Stern appointee and favorite, who spoiled the plan. In August alone, three close Stern followers—all just appointed or promoted to high salary positions in key locals or at SEIU headquarters—were forced to step down due to mishandled funds. The first investigated was Tyrone Freeman, followed by Annelle Grajeda, the new chair, replacing Rosselli, of SEIU's California state council, and Rickman Jackson, the Michigan local leader. Thanks to Stern's personal patronage, all served on the union's executive board. Freeman, Jackson, and Grajeda were among the 60-odd staffers and local officials hand-picked by Stern in June to be part of his administration slate. All were then chosen by the assembled delegates in rubber-stamp fashion. Three months later, Freeman, who still controlled Local 6434 while serving as an SEIU vice president, was the subject of a criminal investigation of racketeering and embezzlement and a related Congressional inquiry by Congressman George Miller (D-Calif.), chair of the House Education and Labor Committee.

As Paul Pringle of the *Los Angeles Times* reported in August 2008 in a stunning investigative series, the U.S. Department of Labor was probing "payments of hundreds of thousands of dollars by the union and a related charity to firms owned by relatives of Freeman and expenditures of similar sums on a golf tournament, restaurants such as Morton's steakhouse, and entertainment companies." [64] The Associated Press estimated the total amount misspent to be $1 million. Freeman's 160,000 SEIU members earned $9 an hour as home care workers. He initially responded to the *Times* revelations in memorable fashion. "Every expenditure has been in the context of fighting poverty," he told Pringle, a struggle that apparently included even his $10,000 tab at the Grand Havana Room, a Beverly Hills cigar bar known for its Hollywood clientele. [65] And $123,000 spent on a golfing tournament at the Four Seasons Resort in Carlsbad. At one point his wife, Pilar Planells, earned more than $50,000 annually as an executive assistant. After leaving the union for the "entertainment" industry, Planells took in $200,000 or more as a producer of videos. Onetime jocks Eric Dickerson and Jackie Slater were also on the take, hosting golfing tournaments and fund-raisers. Within a week of Pringle's story, Freeman took leave of his job "for the duration of the investigation." He was then removed from all positions and continues to face criminal charges.

Rickman Jackson, formerly Freeman's chief of staff at Local 6434, took a "voluntary leave," as well. Jackson had moved from California to Detroit, there becoming president of 50,000-member SEIU Healthcare Michigan. But records revealed that, despite his move to Michigan and Stern-backed political ascendancy in a new local there, Jackson continued to collect $178,000 in salary and benefits from his Los Angeles position. Pringle reported that Jackson received another "$18,000 from SEIU national headquarters for consulting work." And there was the fact that

Jackson's home address in California was listed as the site of a Freeman-run "Long Term Care Housing Corporation," also investigated, an entity, according to Pringle, that "was founded in 2004 as a non-profit but was not granted an IRS tax exemption and had been suspended at one time from doing business in California for failing to file tax returns."[66]

On Labor Day weekend, Pringle reported a third investigation-related "voluntary leave." With Stern's backing, Annelle Grajeda had become head of SEIU's California State Council following Rosselli's forced departure. A former local union staff director, she has never been directly elected by the rank-and-file to any SEIU office. Yet her loyalty to Stern was rewarded in San Juan in the form of new $200,000-a-year paycheck as one of six SEIU international Executive Vice-Presidents. She stepped down from the Council and two other union jobs over accusations that she permitted double- or triple-dipping by her ex-boyfriend, Alejandro Stephens. Stephens was accused of remaining on the payroll of Los Angeles County while collecting "tens of thousands of dollars" from various SEIU entities, including the Grajeda-headed State Council, Grajeda's own 75,000-member local, and the international union.[67]

By mid-August, then, "implosion," Stern's attempt to downsize UHW—by forced transfer to 6434—was for the time being indefensible. Collapse in Southern California demanded new tactics; the "implosion" plan was shelved, though only temporarily. The headquarters' "brain-trust" returned to the drawing boards.

CHAPTER FOUR

"Hands Off Our Union"

Trusteeship was back on the table. In August, Stern named Lerner and three other officials to act as his "Personal Representatives and Monitors" of UHW activity; Lerner was assigned to lead a lawyer-assisted crew of Stern "monitors" to pepper UHW with "information requests" about every conceivable aspect of its daily operations.[68]

Then, on August 25, SEIU headquarters issued a press release announcing "Trusteeship Hearings" to be held in September in San Mateo.

Bill Fletcher, Jr., the former Education Director of the AFL-CIO, recalled in an interview on *Democracy Now!*: "It's ironic... in the spring there were many of us that were concerned that when UHW started raising issues and differences with the Stern leadership, that they were going to be trusted, and we were told, "No, no, no. You're paranoid. This is ridiculous!" Now what did they do? Announce that they were going to have trusteeship hearings with the intention of taking over the local."[69]

UHW members revealed few signs of intimidation, despite, by late summer 2008, months on the receiving end of the SEIU blitzkrieg mailings, robo-calls, personal visits, threats, and offers. In a counter-offensive, tens of thousands of UHW members and supporters took to the streets, packed meetings, petitioned, wrote letters, sent emails, and made phone calls—all in defense not just of UHW but demanding membership participation in democratic unions, membership participation in bargaining, membership rule in the union. They opposed the SEIU's mindless centralism, its sweetheart contracts with employers and its backroom deals with politicians.

The UHW response was spectacular, involving rank-and-file mobilization unparalleled in this period. This uprising, involving tens of thousands of rank-and-file members, began in March in reaction to the first Stern trusteeship letter. Hundreds of UHW members packed the local's Oakland headquarters. In July, at the Manhattan Beach demonstration in Southern California, 5,000 members demonstrated at the "jurisdictional hearings." On September 6, following the UHW's rank-and-file leadership conference, a similar number marched rebelliously through San Jose's center, chanting "Hands off Our Union!" Then, on September 26, trusteeship hearings in San Mateo were greeted by 8,000 UHW members. Inside the hearing room—a grim exhibition hall—more than 1,000 members endured a day of tedious pseudo-legal wrangling in sweltering heat, just to have the minute allowed them. In the hour allotted, 70 members spoke in defense of their union. They spoke with emotion, dignity, and great strength in their beliefs. When the hearing was adjourned, there were still 200 members tenaciously waiting in the lines for a turn at the microphone.

These hearings, held in San Mateo on September 26 and 27, were chaired by 80-year-old Ray Marshall, the secretary of labor under President Carter, now director of a Texas think-tank. They were heavily weighted with the trappings of the courtroom and legality, but in fact bought and paid for by SEIU. Even Marshall's attorneys and staff were on the SEIU payroll.[70] The San Mateo hearings lasted two days, adjourned, reconvened in San Jose in November, and then concluded as scheduled. Interestingly, in spite of the small fortune expended by SEIU on this spectacle, the outcome remained in doubt. Findings were promised for January.

Idle hands in the headquarters? Literally just before the Marshall hearings were concluded, UHW members were hit again. SEIU mailed ballots to all its California healthcare worker members. An election ("advisory only"!) was to be held, the purpose of which was what? To sample the opinion of workers on the possible reorganization of SEIUs entire statewide healthcare operations? The Marshall hearings ended November 15, and UHW members learned of the election two days later. The ballots were to be returned no later than December 11—that is, in less than four weeks' time. This ballot—the "Catch 22" ballot as members called it—offered two choices.

If you are confused, imagine getting this in the mail:

The ballot, asked California healthcare workers if they wanted A) to have 40 percent of UHW members split off into a separate long-term care local, or B) to have all their members subsumed into a new and even larger local. Dan Clawson commented: "Those were the only two choices on the ballot; it was rather like being asked to vote whether you want to be shot in the left knee or both knees."[71] In each case, it goes without saying, the new entities would be led by appointees, selected by Stern in Washington, D.C.

The result of December's sham election was an unqualified repudiation of the SEIU leadership. Out of 309,000 eligible voters, approximately 24,000 SEIU members cast ballots. This means that 92 percent of eligible members boycotted the election. Perhaps just as important, union members presented the Election Officer with petitions protesting the election signed by 80,000 members. These were accompanied by 40,000 formal letters of protest. UHW members presented these letters and petitions in sacks weighing hundreds of pounds. It was an astonishing outpouring of opposition, organized in less than one month.[72]

SEIU, unbelievably, referred to the election results as "a celebration of union democracy." Democracy, Iraq style, that is, or is it now Afghanistan? It presented the results of the election: 20,000 "yes" votes, out of 300,000 eligible— to its Executive Board on January 8 as evidence that the members favored plan "A."[73]

Even in the midst of this storm, UHW continued bargaining; contracts covering 70,000 workers were on the table in 2008. And UHW won victories, including successful negotiations with Catholic Healthcare West. UHW also won elections at O'Connor Woods, Stanford, Marian Medical Center, Sacramento Medical Foundation Clinic, and St. Francis Center; it brought in more hospital workers than the rest of SEIU combined. In late December, UHW ratified contracts at ten nursing homes operated by Kindred Healthcare. The Kindred settlement was its fourth major breakthrough contract in the nursing home industry, part of a decades-long campaign to line up contracts to make significant gains in the nursing home and hospital sectors.

How did SEIU, widely regarded as one of labor's most dynamic and progressive, engender such a mess? How did its culture produce a Tyrone Freeman? In Pringle's *Los Angeles Times* reporting, this "rising star in local labor circles" reminded spectators, accurately, as a free-spending, twenty-first-century SEIU version of Jackie Presser, the Teamster gangster of the 1970s and '80s.[74] Other observers noted a steady drift, in too many SEIU locals, toward the old Teamster brand of plain "business unionism." SEIU leaders collect inflated salaries, tolerate executive board double-dipping, and ignore casual looting of local treasuries, until the membership or media whistle-blowers force them to announce a "clean-up." Implausibly, in August, Stern declared that he was "committed to leading a reform movement in labor."[75] His first objective, apparently, was to crush the reform movement that already existed in his own union, the UHW, then a beacon for SEIU dissidents around the country, before, during, and since the union's Puerto Rico convention.

One of Freeman's early mentors, who asked not to be identified, had this explanation of Freeman's rise and fall (as well as other Stern protégés): "These are folks who did not earn their status, they were handed it and that leads to a dependence on who handed it to you. The union's leadership bench is actually very shallow today ... A person's talent and skill and upward mobility now seem to be in inverse proportion in SEIU."[76]

If loyalty to Stern, rather than competence or honesty, is what leads to rapid career advancement, as it appears to be, then there may be two, three, many Freemans in the union's future. That is because scores of Stern-installed leaders now preside over huge, consolidated locals with few structures for membership accountability or control; many have gotten where they are via initial appointment rather than through membership election. Many have never worked a day in their lives as SEIU members but their local by-laws have been rigged to ensure that they will never easily be replaced by anyone from the rank-and-file.

In Local 6434, for example, a worker wanting to run against Freeman for president is (still) required, within a mere three weeks, to collect and submit the nominating signatures of 4,800 fellow dues-payers! That is an unheard-of hurdle, even in a local with members employed in traditional workplaces. In a union of home-based workers who may not run into five other members in an entire month, it's a guarantee of "presidency for life."

In January 2009, Ray Marshall delivered his report. He held that the original charges against the UHW and its leaders did not warrant trusteeship: not malfeasance;

not conspiring with CNA and other unions; not neglect-
ing contracts; not chilling free speech—none of these
charges were accepted as a basis for SEIU trusteeship. Then,
however, he turned to the issue of the 65,000 long-term care
workers—a subject that was marginal in the long, dreary
and expensive hearings. And, incomprehensibly, he ruled
that UHW had five days to agree to the forced removal of
these workers. If the local failed to agree to this transfer, he
decreed, SEIU could place UHW in trusteeship.[77]

In an extraordinary series of mass meetings on January
25, 5,000 UHW shop stewards and activists showed what
really constituted UHW power: collective action by its
rank-and-file. They voted nearly unanimously to reject
Stern's demands. All three UHW constituencies—hospital workers, nursing home employees, and home healthcare aides—vowed to remain united in UHW and united
as health-care workers, "acute care" and "long-term care"
workers together, one union. On January 26, UHW President
Rosselli offered a last-minute possibility for reconciliation.
He called a press conference and proposed that UHW's
65,000 long-term care workers should be granted the right
to vote on the transfer sought by Stern. Before this balloting, however, he insisted the workers needed guarantees
that Stern's new statewide long-term care local would be
democratically structured and responsive to its projected
240,000 members, unlike SEIU Local 6434 in Los Angeles,
the partner in this yet-to-be-formed "mega-local." At the
time, with both 6434 and UHW under trusteeship—and
three other recently consolidated locals also now operating under Stern-appointed "interim presidents"—about
80 percent of the union's 600,000 members in California
had no elected leaders. Rosselli ended his last press brief-
ing as an elected SEIU official with a carefully worded statement declaring that UHW members would resist trusteeship by all means, up to and including decertification—the

process, sanctioned by the National Labor Relations Act, by which workers can petition to decertify the union, in this case SEIU.

Most often, even in the most conservative U.S. business unions, a transfer on this scale—65,000—would be considered highly unusual, especially if the workers affected had not agreed to it beforehand. Still the UHW compromise was rejected and SEIU—at the earliest moment, January 27, 2009—placed the union in trusteeship. In the SEIU, Stern's directive, the forced transfer of thousands of members—now sanctioned by Marshall—was business as usual. In recent years, Steve Early writes, "No group of dues-payers in America has been treated more like pieces of furniture by top union officials. Under Stern's regime, you can be moved here, there, or anywhere as part of top-down restructuring that always purports to create 'new strength' for workers."[78]

In the two years proceeding Trusteeship, UHW members made a sustained effort to change the way SEIU is run. They borrowed tactics from other reform movements, including Teamsters for a Democratic Union (TDU). Today tens of thousands of workers in California healthcare facilities are taking the fight with Andy Stern and SEIU a step farther, contesting the claim that they have no right to a union of their own choosing. Their bags are packed and they are headed for the door, as soon as federal (or local) labor law permits. These workers made the collective decision to leave SEIU and form NUHW only after the long-threatened trusteeship was put in place. Kaiser Permanente receptionist Eleanor Mendoza explained it to the *Los Angeles Times* at the time this way: "We knew [trusteeship] was coming, and now we have to get real and decertify." According to Mendoza, "You can't have people from the other side of the United States running the union."[79]

CHAPTER FIVE

Occupy!

SEIU expected a ruling in their favor—that's what they paid for.[80] SEIU executive Mary Kay Henry's troops were already on the ground when the findings were announced: several hundred out-of-state SEIU staffers had been dispatched to California as a full-time occupation force. Their mission was to replace the 100 elected UHW executive board members, purge UHW's 500-member staff, seize the local's offices and assets, and inform the employers that they could no longer deal with UHW representatives concerning labor-management issues.

Not so easy. I've forgotten the technical term, what do you call a mob of white people, who, with the police standing by, attack a handful of defenseless people—in this case mostly women of color, a few youngsters—humiliate them, drive them from their home?

The home, the headquarters of UHW, was the target, along with a small number of UHW members. This rear guard occupied their union hall here in Oakland and in all the California offices of UHW, determined not to give up anything without a fight.

This mob—30-, maybe 40-strong—was a nicely dressed group of white men, somewhat out of place for struggling Oakland. It was led by a young, female lawyer, and there were a couple of nasty ex-cops in tow, just in case. They used bolt-cutters to get through the parking-lot gates in back; they smashed their way through a second-floor window and pushed their way to the front. There they opened the doors, let in the rest of the mob and then ended the occupation, evicting members of UHW from their union hall, their house. "Whose House? Our House!"

The Oakland cops arrived just in time to see to it that the newly evicted behaved themselves. They were not impressed, apparently, by the fact that the workers actually had the building's deed in hand. Neither were they concerned that no court had sanctioned this invasion. A Sergeant Kelly assured the workers that everything was just as it should be.

The mob, the "warriors" were staff members and lawyers from SEIU, recruited to do battle from around the country. They came, hundreds in number; they were led personally by SEIU's leadership: Mary Kay Henry, an executive vice president paid $200,000+ a year, pushed her way into the hall. She was assisted by Dave Regan, now trustee, another Executive Vice President, and a $200,000+ guy as well. They were on hand, I guess, just to show that SEIU was serious, but also because the possibility of a little bullying firsthand must have offered them a pleasant diversion from the banalities of Washington, D.C., life. In Regan's case, this seems a career specialization. He had helped orchestrate SEIU's physical assault on the *Labor Notes* Conference.

The SEIU staff seemed to be slumming it—coming to a part of Oakland where grand gentrification schemes languished. Upscale apartments sit empty; the atmosphere of the neighborhood still owes more to the Social Services offices at the end of the street and the Greyhound Bus station around the corner. The rented SUVs and black Audi sedans stood out on deserted Thomas Berkley Way, the site of UHW's headquarters for more than 20 years. The union had long been an important factor in California labor history. Possibly SEIU staff were dressing up—just showing a little respect. Or, again, possibly there was still a dinner party to attend to, or drinks at the Hilton bar.

I spent two days with this "rear guard," UHW members holding the passes, so to speak, as the rest of the old organization UHW spread throughout the state signing up members for their new union.

The mob, of course, preferred to remain nameless. "What is your name? Who are you?" Cold glare. The workers, on the contrary, were quite proud to be there; no one hid in the back. Mell Garcia—a medical assistant with 31 years at Kaiser-Haywood and a chief shop steward—told me, "After Puerto Rico [site of the 2008 SEIU Convention] all bets were off for me, the way they treated us. And now, I can't believe I have the opportunity to make history. We're out from under the 'great dictator'! We can have a union that belongs to us—a union for the members."

By the way, was Andy Stern, "the old Wharton boy" ($250,000+) in the crowd? No, he was in Davos, appropriately, with the World Economic Summit, where "political and business leaders aim to create the foremost global partnerships" Andy Stern likes "partnerships."

Emily Ryan, a licensed clinical social worker and elected shop steward at Kaiser-Folsom, was sitting in, a proud member of the union. She should have been on the new year's UHW executive board; she was elected and would have begun serving in January served had UHW not been wrecked. No more elections now. Regan and Eliseo Medina (yes, $200,000+), yet another executive vice president, were in charge now, appointed co-trustees by Stern.

Ryan believes labor needs a new start—it's been "too cozy with the employers." She's seen the "service model" union and doesn't want it. "Our model is member-driven; it allows us to make our own decisions."

Angela Glasper was the elected chief steward at Kaiser-Antioch. She's been there 20 years. She was a UHW Vice-President and a well-known spokesperson. She's the mother of six. Her daughter Shey, a law student in San Francisco, as well as a younger son, came in and out, bringing food and checking up on mom. I wondered if SEIU staff brought their kids out to California—maybe there was childcare at the Hilton. Glasper went to the Obama inauguration; she took the opportunity to stop by SEIU headquarters. "I can't believe the disrespect. And we [UHW] send them $30 million dollars a year! Every year."

Members started sleeping in the offices early in the week. Rumors had it that the attack would come on Wednesday. Off-duty cops had the building under surveillance. Everyone who came and went had pictures taken. There were never that many members at any one time, but it was important all the same. No one wanted just to abandon the building and "all it stood for." "It wouldn't be right," said Lover Joyce, Kaiser-Walnut Creek. "We couldn't just walk away."

The papers reported that Regan said the occupiers were all UHW staff—this can most likely be explained by the Washington, D.C., company he keeps. SEIU "dues units" had become increasingly unfamiliar to him. A smirking Regan told the *Bay Guardian*, "The police came and we sorted it out." Yes, "sorted out" the people who paid his wages.

The Washington staff probably won't hang around the old Oakland office too long. They don't dress for it. Anyone who's been in an occupation knows you get to know the place too well. In this case the carpets, and the furniture; the office was no place to bring corporate partners. No mahogany conference tables. No leather chairs. No weight room. No portraits of King Andy.

In fact, the hall was dressed up a bit that week. A beautiful, huge banner hung above the front doors declaring "Hands off our Union." But mostly the Oakland office was no frills and a little worse for the wear, an overcrowded place, two floors, lots of cubicles, piles of boxes of files. Not a place for entertaining. There were picket signs, banners, mementos of past strikes and organizing drives, pictures of members in moments of triumph. A history of struggle. SEIU put all the staff on "administrative leave"—told them to stay home, stay away from members and worksites. So the cubicles were left empty, but there were many signs of the people who had worked there, family snapshots pinned above their desks, postcards, children's artwork, political buttons.

In some places there were nice little notes for the replacements to come. One was "When did Eliseo know? 2001?" That was a reference to Medina: the new Trustee. Medina is a generic professional labor leader—a full-timer at unions such as UFW, CWA, and SEIU since the '70s. He led the SEIU in Southern California when Stern appointed Freeman. Medina, apparently, didn't notice much—not a good judge of character.

Ruby Guzman works in a nursing home in San Pablo; she had been a steward for two years, representing 60 workers. She's a single mom, her daughter, a community college student, came along for support. "I was in the Teamsters before this," Guzman told me. "Everything changed when we joined UHW. We were empowered. I negotiated our contract last year. We have the highest standards in California." Guzman is one of the 65,000 long-term care workers to be hijacked from UHW—she would have been sent to Freeman's local. In UHW, she said, "We make $4 more an hour than 6434. We have the right to advocate for our patients—they can't just tell us shut up—and we have the right to take care issues to mediation." "They want us out of UHW... They don't want us in with Kaiser workers because we're too strong that way. We need all healthcare workers united together."

But this was no Alamo. "This is about people, not buildings"—I heard this again and again. Still, as Sonia Minor, elected steward at Kaiser-Martinez, told me, "I'm glad I was there. I'm glad I saw it with my own eyes, the SEIU, the police, the lack of integrity, us together. It made me want to fight more." The real task was getting the new union up and running. But this occupation—and those of all California UHW offices—made it clear to SEIU that they were in for a slog.

There have always been middle-class people in the workers' movements, even Ivy Leaguers and the odd aristocrat. In its own way, it's a tradition to take pride in—class traitors! Whatever. There have even been places for lawyers. Nevertheless, on the Thursday night at eight o'clock, when the first SEIU contingent appeared—led by an impeccably dressed young lawyer, papers in hand, and flanked by six natty white men—the contrast was breathtaking. It's not that Italian mobsters in silk suits would have been more authentic; it's that there, shamelessly, no apologies, no concessions, was the corporate union, twenty-first-century, pure and simple. In the event, they were denied access: "We order you to leave this building!" she said. Response? "No!"

I asked Sal Rosselli why SEIU seemed so disorganized. "Not used to dealing with members," he thought.

It became clear that last night of the occupation that the new (N)UHW could win—the positions were clear, the contrasts sharp, the lynching of UHW ultimately would fail. SEIU's next day evictions would be pyrrhic. I feel like writing it's the bosses vs. the workers, a phrase that makes labor specialists cringe. It's just too nineteenth-century. Anyway, it wasn't the bosses vs. the workers. Ralph Nader was technically wrong to call SEIU a "company union"—it wasn't started by the companies. No, it's the union bosses vs. the workers, but in this very latest corporate incarnation. Sociologically, these are the same people, they represent, really, the same interests. They want to make capital "strong" again, they promise productive workers, "value added." Stern says he doesn't like it when people fight.

These healthcare workers are fighters and as far as I can see, they want out of SEIU because they want to keep fighting. I can imagine (in his reverie) Andy Stern's next, triumphant visit to California, representing 600,000 members, led, almost without exception, by hand-picked lieutenants. Arnold, he dreams, will recognize this. He'll know that here is a man he can work with. Medical care for the twenty-first century: universal, free, no insurance companies. No way. Forget it. Let's make a deal!

CHAPTER SIX

"Healthcare Workers in Control"

When SEIU seized UHW in January 2009, it took control of its assets and fired its 100-member elected executive committee. Medina and Regan, the two appointed trustees, were joined by hundreds of SEIU staff members, a collection of carpetbaggers drafted from bureaucratic baronies across the country. They set out—from the top down—to retake UHW, to "save it" even if the cost was its destruction. (The popular website *Perezstern.blogspot.com* highlighted the trials and tribulations of these hapless individuals).

The drive to build NUHW began at once; the first step was to decertify SEIU—to have members formally state that they chose not to be represented by SEIU. The former staff and members of UHW circulated petitions—hundreds of them—and workers signed them. "Workers *did* so by the thousands and tens of thousands," Dan Clawson observed, "at a rate and in a manner that is unprecedented in the history of the labor movement."[81]

Simultaneously, NUHW was formed. UHW's deposed 100-member Executive Board proposed a new union, backing the demands of the 5,000 stewards and activists who met the weekend before. The former members of UHW set out to rebuild—with no budget, no office, no paid staff. SEIU set about confiscating every possible bit of

UHW property, insisting that every single item belonged to it. Organizers were ordered to return computers, phones, Blackberries, anything and everything.

The NUHW Kaiser campaign, the heart of the new union's strategy, set out to build (rebuild) the union in the workplaces, first by denying SEIU the right to represent Kaiser workers. Kaiser has 32 medical centers and 200 clinics in California. Kaiser origins, like UHW's were also in the 1930s. It is the largest non-profit health plan in the United States. It is the largest healthcare employer in California. It was by far the largest single bargaining unit represented by UHW, nearly 50,000 healthcare workers—dwarfing the next biggest California bargaining unit, Catholic Healthcare West (CHW) that employs 14,000. *Fortune* magazine reports Kaiser's revenues last year at $37.8 billion; it is the fifth largest private company in the nation, serving 8.7 million members.[82]

The Kaiser contract was the result of years of shop-floor conflict, strikes, and contested collective bargaining (and the "partnership"—now in tatters). "In the early 1990s, our union had strikes against Kaiser in Oregon, Denver, and Los Angeles. We were at war with the corporation," Rosselli told the *Chronicle*.[83] Kaiser towers over the California healthcare industry. UHW's Kaiser members enjoyed the best wages and benefits in the country. Moreover, the Kaiser contract was used to leverage up other contracts, not just in hospitals but also in nursing homes and for home care workers.

SEIU could seize the property of these workers; they could not, however, confiscate their experience. At Kaiser, the experience was one of building a powerful workplace organization. Angela Glasper described the old UHW at Kaiser:

> In our organization, workers made all the major
> decisions, so the workers in a department had the

right to elect who their steward will be. They also had the right to unelect the stewards, if the stewards didn't represent their interests.

The stewards, together in a facility, comprised a Stewards' Council. The Stewards' Council made policy and other types of decisions at the facility level. So the stewards, say in the hospital division, those who worked in the acute care setting, got together at least four times a year to discuss strategy and make decisions about the direction of the hospital division. All together, all the stewards in the union, gathered together at least once per year at a leadership conference to determine the direction of the union overall for the coming year, to review what accomplishments, what the successes and failures had been in the preceding twelve months and to lay out a vision for the next twelve months or longer.

Our stewards were strongly represented on the UHW Executive Committee, they were probably the majority. And that way the information in the union flows not just from the top down but more importantly from the bottom up.[84]

On February 26, 2009, these workers realized an historic achievement: they filed representation petitions asking the NLRB to conduct decertification election (to rescind SEIU's legal recognition) at Kaiser. These petitions were signed by more than 50 percent of all of California's 50,000 of Kaiser's SEIU-represented healthcare workers. The petitions represented, starkly, the desire of these California healthcare workers to leave SEIU. Or, more precisely, their desire to maintain their own union, NUHW, which they recognized as the only legitimate successor to UHW.

This petition campaign was the culmination of one phase in the drive to form the NUHW—but it was an astonishing accomplishment. It was all the more impressive as it represented just the core of an ongoing campaign that, in twelve weeks following the creation of NUHW, enlisted workers at 380 California healthcare facilities. More than 100,000 workers—the majority of the members of SEIU's once flagship local, UHW—had rejected SEIU and petitioned for recognition of NUHW as their union. This in less than one month! Ten thousand home care workers in Fresno filed the following week.

John Borsos believes that this was the largest decertification drive ever. Astonishingly, it was conducted entirely by healthcare workers themselves and the fired former elected staff of UHW. This surely bears repeating: the signatures were collected in less than one month by healthcare workers seeking recognition, an entirely volunteer-run project, aided by a handful of fired staff, as well as others who had resigned in protest, or out of loyalty, or just because of the values that attracted them to union work in the first place.

On April 25, 2009, the NUHW founding convention was held in San Francisco—an event of great enthusiasm.[85] The convention site was the magnificent Everett Middle School in the Mission—just a short walk, we were reminded, from where the union, then Local 250, was founded in the tumultuous 1930s. Seven hundred workers attended, nearly all the formerly elected shop stewards of UHW, plus remaining staff.

Glasper opened the meeting, followed by Mike Casey, his union also embroiled in a bitter national conflict with SEIU. "Thank you for standing up," he told NUHW members. "We will look back on this day as when we got the movement back on track." He denounced Andy Stern as a "misleader"—a man who promoted the notion that concessions were the "tough decisions" unions must make. "I call it selling out!" Casey concluded that this "was our generation's chance to make labor relevant—or be consigned to the dust bin."

Rosselli, interim president of the new union, outlined a two-year perspective, a "foundation for growth" based on building NUHW "organizing committees in the workplace." He acknowledged setbacks, in particular the long delays at the NLRB. But "the worst case scenario," he predicted, would be elections at Kaiser next year: "There will be a vote in 2010, and there is nothing SEIU can do to stop it." The Convention voted to adopt a provisional constitution and by-laws; guaranteeing "our right to elect our co-workers to represent us in contract negotiations, and our right to elect stewards and officers." Changes made it easier for members to run for office; the number of signatures needed was reduced to 25. Dues were lowered dues to 1.5 percent (from SEIU-UHW's 2 percent dues rate), with no initiation fee. It elected a founding committee of leaders—the committee is made up of almost all the same rank-and-file leaders who were elected to lead SEIU-UHW before Stern's takeover. In the afternoon, there were divisional meetings—hospitals, long-term care, public sector, as well as practical sessions devoted to helping workers survive in hostile settings, where members routinely faced SEIU retaliation, management harassment and the collusion of human relations staff and SEIU.

The decertification petitions had just been the start; it is one thing to petition the NLRB, it is another to force the agency to act responsibly and offer rank-and-file workers a fair hearing and fair elections—"a free choice." The NLRB is the agency within the U.S. government charged with conducting elections for labor union representation and investigating charges of unfair labor practices. It has a five-person board and a general counsel, all appointed by the president; they oversee regional offices and staff. The agency's origins, in the 1930s, lie in the National Labor Relations

Act (the New Deal Wagner Act, 1935) that made trade union-ism legal, allowing workers in most of the private sector to create labor unions, engage in collective bargaining and take part in strikes, as well as other forms of concerted activity in support of their demands. The employers never really accepted it, even after passage of the Taft-Hartley Act in 1948, though it has rarely lived up to its pro-labor reputa-tion. It does, however, offer procedures for representation, fair bargaining and an appeals process for workers and their unions. At best it is a cumbersome and time-consum-ing process for defending workers' rights; at worst it has reflected the politics of the party in power and of course this had been the case in the Reagan-Bush era.

The NLRB is contested terrain. Unions can petition for elections. Employers can oppose them. The employers can then wheel in their lawyers, their specialists and consult-ants—as they do whenever they can. Then come the delays, the postponements, the recesses, the appeals. All the while, on the job, the struggle continues. And, while the workers await the vote, however long delayed, the employers are free to intimidate, harass, and often terminate the very people who seeking protection. Union organizers are all too familiar with law firms and the corporate consultants that specialize in this, as well as with the countless "dirty tricks" within the employers' arsenals. In this case, the NLRB, at SEIU's insist-ence, has ruled in almost every case so far that elections are only allowed in "open periods"—restricted periods such as when contracts are expired. As a result California healthcare workers are in effect held hostage by the SEIU, a condition sanctioned by the NLRB.

The "Employee Free Choice Act" (EFCA) now before Congress is organized labor's attempt to remedy these fail-ings by amending the National Labor Relations Act in the hope of making it easier for workers to form, join or assist labor organizations and to provide for penalties for unfair labor practices, particularly in organizing efforts. EFCA would require, for example, the NLRB to certify a bargaining representative without directing an election if a majority of the bargaining unit employees signed cards, the card-check process. EFCA is of course vehemently opposed by business because it would simplify efforts by workers to unionize and negotiate first contracts.

Stern himself, in a *USA Today* interview on this subject, was right on: "Union members can opt out of unions by checking a card so they should be able to opt in that way as well."[86] There we have it! Workers "can opt out of unions!" So let the workers decide! Why not free elections for the Kaiser workers? No one doubts the outcome, clearly not California's Kaiser workers. Mell Garcia, Kaiser-Hayward: "We're building NUHW because it's the only way to protect the gains that Kaiser workers have won over the past 65 years. Membership power is the way to power at work."[87] Shayne Silva, a psychiatric technician at Alta Bates Summit in Oakland, says, "We hope Andy Stern and SEIU will walk away and leave us alone."[88]

No such luck. Dave Regan told the *Los Angeles Times* he will fight "every step of the way."[89] And indeed the obstructions followed. Michelle Ringuette, a national spokesperson for SEIU, charged that the petitions were not valid. She said members didn't understand the issues. She said workers were being coerced. NUHW, she said, is guilty of "raiding" (she would know).[90] The lawyers got to work; the NLRB announced it must investigate. Regan began concessionary talks with Kaiser. Stern announced a new SEIU-wide committee to bargain with Kaiser—a stacked committee where California's members can be outvoted by representatives from Colorado and Oregon, state organizations that together represent only 4,000 members.

This, of course, is just what the employers do: war on all fronts and don't let the workers choose! It is the very reason that unions are pressing for passage of EFCA. It is also exactly what we were warned SEIU would do—and—also that SEIU would be good at it. The predicted stall began and, as the clock ran, SEIU began a search and destroy operation in the workplaces—hospitals, nursing homes and clinics across California. SEIU imitated the employers on the shop floor, their project was to dismantle the old UHW. They attacked the human infrastructure of the unions. Stewards were fired, bargaining committees disbanded. SEIU-UHW staff used intimidation, harassment, and in collusion with Kaiser and the other employers there came discipline, even dismissals. The people who were and are the union became the front line in a guerrilla war. Here are examples of what they faced:

- On February 1 Inez Moreno, a shop steward at 269-bed Mercy Hospital in Bakersfield, received a phone call from an SEIU organizer. Moreno was told not to circulate petitions. If she refused, the organizer would call the hospital's Human Resources Department on Monday and have her terminated. "She said I had been stripped of my stewardship... She thinks she can call me and treat me like nothing."

- On February 9 Maria Garcia, a certified nursing assistant and elected shop steward at 99-bed Bay Point Healthcare Center in Hayward, was fired for circulating a petition to join NUHW. Her boss phoned her and said that if Medina didn't approve of the petition, she would be fired. Days later, he terminated Garcia, who is an immigrant from Mexico and a single mother of three children.

- On February 11 Angelica Valerio, a certified nursing assistant and member of the elected Windsor Healthcare bargaining committee, was suspended from her job—nine others received written warnings— for refusing to let an SEIU staffer bargain their contract. A majority of Windsor workers had already petitioned to disaffiliate from SEIU. With 29 nursing homes, for-profit Windsor Healthcare is one of the largest nursing home chains in California.

- On February 23 three SEIU organizers arrived at 1,049-bed California Pacific Medical Center, Sutter Health's flagship hospital located in San Francisco. Two of the facility's elected rank-and-file leaders, Helen York-Jones and Porfirio Quintano, asked the SEIU organizers to leave their hospital. York-Jones is a Cashier and 40-year employee who was a former elected member of SEIU-UHW's Executive Board. Quintano, a housekeeper with ten years on the job, was a steward and an elected member of the union's bargaining committee. The two leaders told the SEIU staffers that a majority of the hospital's workers had already submitted petitions to disaffiliate from SEIU, and they did not want SEIU organizers in their facility. The organizers reported them to the hospital's Human Resources Department. Two days later York-Jones and Quintano received calls from Sutter management announcing that they had been placed on unpaid investigatory leave.[91]

The path chosen by UHW/now NUHW activists is not the easy one. UHW leaders predicted the massive retaliation in this all-too-familiar form. SEIU always has been willing to use its huge resources and makes no secret of its ability to resort to trusteeship to keep unhappy members held hostage. UHW is far from the first SEIU local to be placed in trusteeship. Since Stern became president, SEIU has removed elected local union officers (replacing them with appointed trustees or "interim presidents") in nearly 80 affiliates. Percentage-wise and in absolute numbers, Stern's trusteeship stats put him in a league of his own in organized labor.

The word "decertification" always sends a shiver down the spine of the union bureaucrat. The idea of replacing an incumbent union—no matter how bad—is almost universally opposed; even critics tend to view this as a strategic dead-end, more, a very dangerous exercise in "disunity." Yet, elsewhere in the world, it is widely accepted that forming a rival union (or joining a competing labor federation) is a fundamental expression of workers' "freedom of assoc-iation." Trade unionists and intellectuals, especially those who favor the Employee Free Choice Act to aid union organ-izing, should reconsider this and ask how they can recon-cile "employee free choice" and a belief that dissatisfied dues-paying workers should not have the option of joining a new labor organization? Particularly if the existing one doesn't even allow them the right to choose their own local union or its leaders?

Nevertheless, the fact is that Stern is far from unde-feated. In 2000, SEIU lost a quarter of its total member-ship in Ontario after workers there revolted against Stern's attempted consolidation of eight local unions into one. SEIU was already facing member backlash at the lack of responsiveness and democratic participation. Stern's prov-ince-wide merger plan met opposition from both members and local executive boards across Ontario. Just before a general membership vote to abandon SEIU, Stern placed all Ontario locals under trusteeship. But the election went ahead and, the workers with near unanimous support, the workers voted to leave SEIU; immediately, the Canadian Auto Workers (CAW) raided SEIU's Ontario bargaining units, eventually winning decertification votes in 180 units, representing 14,000 members.[92]

In 2002 and 2003, Rhode Island janitors, campus main-tenance workers, and librarians represented by SEIU Local 134 were told they had to merge with a Boston-based building service workers local that Stern had recently put in trusteeship. When the vast majority signed a peti-tion to keep their own local, their wishes were ignored; members responded by starting to form an independent union, the United Service and Allied Workers-Rhode Island (USAW-RI). By 2007, almost all of 134's original bargaining units had voted to switch from SEIU to USAW-RI, when their contracts expired or pre-contract expiration "open periods" enabled workers to file labor board petitions to decertify. In the meantime, USAW-RI managed to organize 150 new members at the Providence Library, while fending off a costly, harassing lawsuit filed by SEIU against Local 134 officers who were accused of breaching their "fiduciary duty" to the international union.

Post-trusteeship litigation got messy when 2,000 Bay Area janitors tried to bail out of SEIU in the summer of 2004. In response to yet another Stern take-over, they formed United Service Workers for Democracy (USWD) to oust their old bargaining representative, SEIU Local 87, and win the right to negotiate with San Francisco cleaning service contractors. SEIU flooded downtown office buildings with out-of-town organizers—just like the Stern loyalists now occupying SEIU-UHW—but the janitors still won their decertification vote by a two-to-one margin. Undeterred, SEIU seized Local 87's property, sued USWD's lawyer, and tried to thwart management recognition of the new union—the strategy now pursued against NUHW.

Can NUHW do what USAW-RI, SEIU's Canadian dissidents, and other groups have already done, albeit on a smaller scale? There are people with years of experience in healthcare organizing who think that NUHW will fare better than most defectors. One is Jerry Brown, the now retired, longtime president of SEIU's 20,000-member healthcare affiliate in Connecticut and Rhode Island. A former member of Stern's international executive board, Brown praises Rosselli for standing up "for the rights of members to determine their own future and run their own union, to fight for better standards and engage in militant action if they choose to."[93]

According to Brown, "Stern and other SEIU leaders have now centralized all important national bargaining and organizing in D.C. and effectively neutered the power of the members to bargain with their bosses. The result will be and has been already a series of sweetheart contracts that take away or severely limit the right to strike and other traditional union rights like seniority, workplace grievances, and numerous other boss inspired limitations." [94]

To Brown and other SEIU leaders, the UHW takeover has been a painful, "horrible development for SEIU and the entire labor movement." Once Stern's colleague and discreet in-house critic, Brown now says publicly that "Stern et al are a disgrace and we should mobilize to help the new union and the thousands of courageous UHW members who have stood up to SEIU." [95]

CHAPTER SEVEN

"We Can Get Involved"

Perhaps more than any other union, SEIU has made a principle of centralized, top-down decision making. It has maligned membership rights and the election of representatives; it has belittled the idea of workers' participation, in theory as well as practice. In its centralism, "one voice," the SEIU leadership substitutes itself for the membership, in its "one strategy" it implicitly substitutes itself for the entire labor movement if not the working class. Oblivious to the history of the movement's unpredictably, its spontaneity, SEIU's perspectives are mechanical in the extreme.

Unfortunately, there are others in the labor movement who share these views, but few with the shamelessness of Stern and his regime. And SEIU, alas, has its supporters, including in the universities and amongst the "experts" who staff the country's academic labor centers, a small chorus of academics who cheer SEIU on.[96]

In the years of Stern's ascent, it has been common, in seminars and on the agendas of academic conferences, to see listed speakers and panels debating the topic "union democracy." The 1999 Yale conference, hosted by Scholars, Artists and Writers for Social Justice (SAWSJ), featured such a session; the question was debated, pro or con, "Are democratic unions the best way to mobilize militant workers?" This panel addressed this "*controversial* question from the perspective of labor historians, union organizers and democratic theorists." Stern, while not on this panel, was a keynote speaker at the conference.[97]

The debate, ten years on, still with SEIU at the center, has undermined fundamental beliefs, including what ought to be the self-evident notion of the indispensability of democracy within the workers' movement. Historian Steve Fraser once cynically suggested that union democracy was a non-issue, a fetish of an insignificant Left, when not a weapon of the Right. He added, approvingly: "many labor leaders secretly believe and practice what one of them openly confessed back in the 1920s: 'As a democracy no union would last six months.'"[98] This has taken its toll on the movement—as has the SEIU checkbook; rare is the labor center, publication or project that is not in debt to Stern, one way or another. Nevertheless, this will change; it has already. This past summer, hundreds of academics, most still unwilling to support NUHW, signed a letter condemning SEIU raids on UNITE HERE. Stanley Aronowitz replied to Fraser in the '90s debate and his answer still stands: "When unions deprive the rank-and-file of choice, when leaders favor mobilization but not participation, they succeed only in driving a deeper nail in labor's coffin."[99]

SEIU nationally was not the scene of '60s and '70s movements, but it moved center-stage in 1995; its President John Sweeney led the "New Voice" team that successfully forced Lane Kirkland, President of the AFL-CIO, to step down, then defeated his nominee, Secretary-Treasurer Thomas Donahue. Sweeney's election was highly unusual in U.S. labor history: seldom are incumbent administrations replaced. This was an important achievement but one with few memorable results. But one should be acknowledged. Sweeney's election was greatly helped by the 1991 victory of Ron Carey, the reformer who became Teamsters president, in part with the aid of Teamsters for a Democratic Union. Sweeney helped underwrite the 1997 UPS workers strike. The 190,000 workers there defeated the world's largest transportation corporation. The victory was praised by Sweeney: "You can make a million house calls, run a thousand television commercials, stage a hundred strawberry rallies, and still not come close to doing what the UPS strike did for organizing."[100] The UPS example, however, was not to be followed.

Stern followed Sweeny as President of SEIU, and then defied Sweeny's rule in the AFL-CIO in 2005. This time the result was not a new leadership but a new Federation, "Change to Win (CtW)," an unlikely coalition of SEIU, the Teamsters Union, UNITE HERE, the United Food and Commercial Workers, the Laborers Union, the Carpenters (disaffiliated in 2009) and the United Farm Workers, with a very foggy program: "United to Win: 21st Century Plan to Build New Strength for Working People." There is no doubt that an impatient Stern wanted change. He seemed, on the surface to have set a progressive course. He genuinely seems to have believed that the nation's service sector workers were there for the taking. But there was little discussion of any of this, little debate in the run-up to the split. Few understood the principles, if any, of the new federation; fewer still could foresee how these would inform the issues that now plague CtW (bargaining, organizing, jurisdictions). CtW hit the ground running, however; it claimed six million members, anointed itself the vanguard of change, promising reorganization, centralization and, above all, growth.

Sweeny, just retired as President of the AFL-CIO, is a middle-of-the road labor leader, a man who, if anything, looks nostalgically back to the big labor days of '50s business unionism. Stern brought business unionism up to date. *The Wall Street Journal* finds "Mr. Stern at ease with CEOs and in the media limelight. His sentences come seasoned with business phrases." The new federation would "grow the labor movement" through increased "market share" and "value-added integration" and a steady stream of blitz-krieg campaigns and false advertising. An admiring Steven Greenhouse, writing in the *New York Times*, observed "Mr. Stern's approach resembles that of a corporate chief executive…"[101] Stern inspired the union's brand—the purple shirt. "Partnership" is a watchword and class collaboration is a badge of honor.[102]

Kim Moody calls the SEIU "bureaucratic corporate unionism."[103] It is a union run not just as a business, but according to the norms of a modern corporation. The largely appointed "team" of national officers is at its core; a small army of full-time staffers carries out the line. It has been centralized with a vengeance; Local 1199, the New York hospital workers union, is now the 240,000-member 1199 Eastern District, representing workers as far afield as Baltimore. SEIU's leaders, none more so than Stern and his second-in command Anna Burger, have been elevated to cult-like figures, as have lieutenants, regardless of experience and achievement. Central to SEIU's strategy of "growth at any cost" is what Moody describes as "the politics of the deal." The "deal" is hardly new in U.S. labor history; the old barons were quite good at it. "Punish your enemies, reward your friends," admonished the late Samuel Gompers. The recent history of the SEIU, however, is truly mind-boggling. Here are examples:

In 2002 Dennis Rivera—then President of New York's 1199 and long a darling of progressive union watchers—concluded a deal with the conservative Governor George Pataki. In return for electoral support, Pataki would push through a bill raising wages for state healthcare workers. The bill was passed; Pataki won the election, defeating African-American Democrat Carl McCall.

In 2004 SEIU gave now-disgraced Illinois Governor Rod Blagojevich $800,000 in return for collective bargaining rights for 37,000 home healthcare workers. Now the union is knee-deep in the governor's senate-seat-for-sale scheme. SEIU gave Blagojevich $1.8 million in two runs for governor.

In 2007 *The Seattle Times* exposed a secret agreement between SEIU Local 775 and operators of for-profit nursing homes. The companies involved pledged to "bless" the union's organizing efforts in exchange for a ten-year agreement, in which the union promised no strikes and agreed to let the nursing-home operators, not the union or workers, decide which homes are offered up for organizing. The union also agreed not to try organizing more than half of a particular company's non-union homes. This agreement is still in effect.[104]

In 2007 in California, Andy Stern personally intervened in the state's debate on healthcare reform. He brushed aside the wishes of the California section of the SEIU, as well as political supporters of a universal system and engaged in direct talks with Governor Arnold Schwarzenegger, joining him in promoting a bill backed by business and the insurance industry.

In June 2008 Puerto Rican teachers, members of the Federación de Maestros de Puerto Rico (FMPR), defeated a government sponsored attempt to break their union, which represents 42,000 teachers and is known for its militant support of teachers and students. Backed by the SEIU, and supported by Governor Aníbal Acevedo Vilá, the SPM (Sindicato Puertorriqueno de Maestros) was soundly rejected by teachers who called it a "company union" and accused SEIU of collusion. Vilá was the honored guest at SEIU's June convention in Puerto Rico, where he was personally introduced by his close friend, Dennis Rivera, now national chief of SEIU's healthcare division.

This is no way to run a union.

The desperate desire for growth, "density," the demand to grow now, fast, as well as the vision of the world transformed have (for too many) swept aside issues such as members' rights. Just consider this example: SEIU's policy of telephone service centers, "member resource centers," alternatives to democratic networks of shop stewards. Shop stewards are the representatives of the workers in the workplace. Stern suggested to British counterparts that they were a "bad idea." Yet shop stewards, time and again in labor's history, have been the workers' first line of defense, as well as their advanced guard.

If the wish to eliminate stewards from the shop floor reveals Stern's contempt for the most immediate concerns of the worker, the quadrennial San Juan convention was a public spectacle of SEIU's corporate project. The convention, a lavish gathering of 3,000 mainlanders, was by all accounts a caricature of centralism, under the tight control of yellow-vested "sergeants at arms"—a charade down to the last detail. Properly credentialed SEIU visitors had to be bused to and from their hotels to convention meetings—the whole "convention center district" was cordoned off with metal barricades. The convention hall itself was surrounded by police, including muscle-bound, jack-booted, club-swinging San Juan riot cops (the notorious "shock police"), sent in to defend the convention from militant teachers, members of the FMPR chanting "Stop union raids!"

The SEIU in its internal wars demands "majority rule." It denounces collusion! Talk about collusion! Juan Gonzalez accused SEIU of "arrogant and colonialist" behavior, calling SEIU's attempted undermining of FMPR a "shameful betrayal of solidarity."[105] In the exchanges that followed the Puerto Rico Convention and the Freeman scandals, Ken Paff—for years a champion of democracy in the Teamsters—remarked, "When your union is less democratic than the

Teamsters, you have to look in the mirror and say, 'What happened?'"[106] Benson added, "When a rare independent leader with a following and ample resources resists, like Sal Rosselli has done, the alarm sounds: Not good enough to answer him; he must be crushed." Furthermore, a younger generation in the labor movement is "now being suffocated by an ideology that sees labor's future dependent upon an authoritarian, manipulative leadership..."[107]

NUHW has its supporters, many, given the circumstances.[108] Dolores Huerta, the farm workers leader, a co-founder of the United Farm Workers, testified in favor of UHW at the Marshall hearings. She did this despite enduring an hour on the phone with former farm worker colleague Eliseo Medina, who vainly pleaded with her not to give evidence. Huerta recalled that she had worked with UHW for years—so much so that she deserved "an honorary membership." She continued,

> I've known the people in UHW. Many of the staff
> have been on various campaigns. I've always known
> them to be people with a lot of integrity, a lot of
> commitment, very, very hard workers in terms
> of the organizing that they do in reaching out to
> their members, and a lot of involvement from
> the membership. And my impression has always
> been it's a very democratic organization, a very
> open organization that has a lot of commitment to
> organizing, and making better benefits and wages for
> the workers.[109]

San Francisco County Supervisors, all seven of them, joined a rally in support of UHW in November 2008, as did hundreds of local community leaders and union officers; they signed letters of support and issued appeals to Stern: urging a peaceful resolution, offering mediation, opposing a hostile takeover. The rally in the San Francisco Plumbers

Hall a year later was supported by leaders of UNITE HERE, UFCW, the firefighters, the Sailors Union of the Pacific, as well as political and community leaders including John Burton, the longtime California Democrat Party leader. The educators' May Day letter was followed by an appeal from 50 prominent California educators and intellectuals.[110] On November 21, 2008, a day-long conference was held at the University of California–Berkeley. Originally designed to present for discussion both sides to the dispute, when SEIU refused to respond to repeated invitations, the conference became a seminar on healthcare unionism and trade union democracy. Participants included scholars and activists from multiple UC campuses, state universities, and community colleges, as well as labor activists and a contingent of working members of UHW. There were, however, no representatives, despite repeated invitations, of the labor centers at UC–Berkeley and UCLA. The widely held conclusion, at the end of the day, was that the UHW was not just to be defended; it was to be supported as offering a positive way forward for an embattled labor movement.

Since the Berkeley Conference, support meetings, receptions and rallies have been held in dozens of places, including, Boston, New York, Chicago, Seattle, Portland, Vermont, Santa Rosa, Los Angeles, Washington, D.C., and Northampton. The very first meeting, hosted in Berkeley by Retort, heard a first-hand expose of SEIU's oppositional research—hired researchers building the case against UHW. A participant explained how this project was carried out—in New York, in the office of Local 1199, revered by progressives, organized by Amy Gladstein, 1199's organizing director. The informant spoke in defiance, we were told, of a confidentiality oath administered by the barrister herself. Three meetings in New York and New England, following the 2009 Left Forum, collected $17,000. The meeting in Seattle in August 2009 was held in the King County Labor

Temple, where more than 100 people packed the union hall. The November 2009 meeting, held in the offices of the United Teachers of Los Angeles, was attacked by egg- and bottle-throwing SEIU staff and bused in members. A UTLA vice president was among those hit. These meetings represent a modest and growing national network, one that continues to grow and plans to facilitate the organization of volunteers expected to come to California for the summer's elections.

It remains obvious that there are still legions of good union members within SEIU, doing, no doubt, wonder- ful work. I am certain also that UHW was, and NUHW is, far from perfect. The fact remains that UHW, a militant, democratic, growing union, was wrecked by SEIU, and it is a disservice to the movement to remain silent in such circumstances. Why is there not more support, in particu- lar from trade unionists outside California? And from the nation's progressive teachers and intellectuals? There will be many reasons on offer, but a telling one is that Dolores Huerta was not the only one to have received a warning phone call. SEIU systematically pursued the signers of the May Day letter, arm-twisting, contesting, cajoling, mixing promises with threats, and, regrettably, the truth is that many ran for cover. The same can be said for university labor centers where the response to UHW has most often been, "We can't get involved." This silence of the scholars, this feigned neutrality, is explained in part, one guesses, by crude self-interest, also perhaps by the inherent conserva- tism of their setting, the modern university, with its usual moral apathy. In too many places, when SEIU is concerned critical thinking seems not to apply—it might "help the bosses," we don't "meddle in the internal affairs." SEIU refuses to discuss, let alone debate the issues in this conflict; it limits discussion to private, invitation-only informa- tion sessions. Still, it remains the patron of many: pay to play, reward your friends, and punish your enemies. There are, of course, centers and scholars dependent financially on the generosity of SEIU (and other unions), generosity, however, that comes with strings. Is this understandable? Possibly. Still, it is a relationship that begs the question of the mission of the labor programs and their supporters on the campuses.

And the employers? SEIU (again) has made their day. "We're going to make SEIU the poster child for the campaign against the Employee Free Choice Act," says Sarah Longwell, the spokeswoman for the Center for Union Facts, a right-wing, pro-corporate think tank.[111]

CHAPTER EIGHT

"Fresno—SEIU's Vietnam"

The first test on the ground in the California war took place in June in the sprawling Central Valley city of Fresno, where in June 2009 10,000 home healthcare workers won the chance to choose a union to represent them. The election came as the result of petitions signed in two weeks in February by 2,500 Fresno County home care workers—far more than the 1,500 signatures required. These were delivered by NUHW supporters to Fresno County authorities on March 1, in accordance with the requirements of the Public Employees Relations Act. While home care workers often technically work for the private individuals they care for, funding comes from the counties and the state; hence the workers, considered public employees, are not covered by the labor board.

On Tuesday, May 5, the Public Employee Relations Board recognized the workers' petitions and set the election for June 1–15. This represented an important victory for healthcare workers—a breakthrough and an opportunity that until then had been successfully blocked by SEIU lawyers, and Kaiser and other large healthcare employers.

While both unions sent organizers into Fresno County, for SEIU it was "shock and awe." SEIU deployed nearly 1,000 full-time, paid staff, mostly out-of-state "warriors" armed with lawyers, SUVs and credit cards, to be set up in the best motels Fresno has to offer (sadly a step down from Hiltons of the Bay Area and Southern California they'd become accustomed to). In the end, it was estimated that SEIU spent $10 million on the Fresno front. NUHW, still only months old, its members' collective assets seized by SEIU in the January trusteeship, relied on worker organizers, Fresno homecare workers, member volunteers and former UHW staff.

It was fitting that this battle involved home healthcare workers—the poorest on the healthcare occupational ladder; most often without benefits; who care for the poor, the aging, and the disabled. These "clients" are often family members or neighbors; thus both the workers and their clients live and work the mean streets of the nation, quite removed from any California Dream—certainly in the Central Valley. "Despite such socially necessary labor," write Jennifer Klein and Eileen Boris, healthcare historians, the home care workers' wages are "lower than all other jobs in healthcare with the exception of janitors." [112] Still, home healthcare is one of the fastest growing sectors of the industry. And it has been a key target in SEIUs "organizing" campaigns designed for union growth—increased "density" (and "dues units") at all costs. Consequently home healthcare workers are often at the center of the wheeling and dealing, objects in the back-room bargaining of Stern and his regime of appointed lieutenants, as in the Illinois Blagojevich scandals.

The Fresno workers, UHW members in good-standing well before trusteeship, would be among the 65,000 transferred (without a vote) to scandal-ridden Local 6434 and the tender mercies of its SEIU trustees. Yet, these workers, including those in Fresno, were among the best paid home care workers in the country, their wages were the result in part of UHW's ability to leverage up standards towards those at the top, the hospital workers. The SEIU plan, in contrast, was to segregate California's long-term care providers into a massive statewide local, to be led by Stern appointees. Interestingly, this transfer has yet to happen and Fresno's home care workers, along with thousands of other California healthcare workers, remain captive in the "zombie" SEIU-UHW.

The fundamental issues in the Fresno contest were clear—the NUHW, if it won the election, would maintain and build on standards fought for and won by members of the wrecked UHW, including contesting recent Fresno County's proposed wage cuts, while fighting for healthcare benefits for all, and challenging state caps on wages and benefits and a system that perpetuates for these workers a cycle of permanent poverty. On the other hand, by May SEIU had already lost in arbitration and conceded the County's wage cut demands. Still, Stern predicted that Fresno would be the "death knell" for NUHW. It is far more likely that an SEIU win will be the "death knell" for the home care workers.

SEIU sent in staff from out of state, led by Rebecca Malberg, a D. C. staffer who didn't know the contract, had never handled a grievance, and never witnessed an arbitration. SEIU refused to allow the members' local bargaining team to attend arbitration hearings. After an arbitration ruling in favor of the County, the SEIU refused to share the findings with members, but it still called the secret contract a "victory."

In early January 2009, Medina—then still an SEIU vice president assigned to Texas—wrote to me suggesting that I failed to grasp the issues involved in the SEIU-UHW dispute. Seizing, I suspect, on my habitation in cushy Northern California, he wrote: "Much of my current organizing is now taking place in the South and Southwest, which is as far from [San Francisco] in culture and worker power, as you can get." This, of course, reflected the SEIU mantra of the moment, most often elaborated by Lerner. The charge was that the then dissident UHW was content to confine its efforts to the easy places, like "...San Francisco that traditionally have had relatively strong labor movements and friendly political environments" rather than taking on, with Medina and company, the real work in the "more difficult regions where workers face even greater obstacles." [113]

Where do these people live? I know Medina's been to Fresno—many times, I suspect. He began his career in California as a young organizer of farm workers, working the Valley in the heyday of César Chávez and the United Farm Workers. Fresno is 170 miles from Oakland, less than a three-hour drive. It is a poor city. Residents were shocked to learn of a 2006 Brookings Institution report on the nation's fifty largest cities that ranked the city number one in concentrated poverty (number four in overall poverty), based on a study of the country's fifty largest cities—in fact ahead even of pre-Katrina New Orleans as the city with the deepest neighborhood poverty. [114]

Fresno, with 500,000 residents in a metropolitan area of a million, follows in the California pattern; it is in reality two cities, the home care workers live in the one that is comprised of Latinos and new immigrants. The latter still come in large numbers for jobs washing dishes, work in the packing houses and in the fields, and the healthcare industry, which is, as elsewhere, is thriving. Many live in the slums of the south side—sprawling neighborhoods of small homes, trailer parks, and apartment complexes, with of course, everything that comes with poverty. They breathe some of the worst air in California; Fresno is ranked number two by the American Lung Association in short term particle pollution. [115] It has been hammered by the recession. Unemployment in the valley cities is the highest in the state: Fresno has 16.5 percent, Modesto 17.2 percent, Merced 18.3 percent, Yuba City 18.8 percent, and Sacramento 12.4 percent. [116] It is in the top ten in everything we don't want, resulting in all the usual health hazards. The Central Valley is one of the four super-centers of the sub-prime scandal—Fresno ranks fourteenth in foreclosures nationwide.

Nevertheless, the power of large-scale agribusiness persists and Fresno remains, like much of the Valley, conservative, dominated by white republicans. In early June the representatives of these people on the county Board of Supervisors, citing of course California's permanent budget crisis, proposed cutting home care workers' pay by almost 75 cents an hour—from $10.25 (with 60 cents an hour for healthcare coverage) to $9.50. A complicated formula in California's 2004 "Aging with Dignity" Act sets a cap on home care workers' wages, but the process begins with the County's contribution and the union negotiates with the County first. These proposed cuts, and the disaster they represent, continue to haunt Fresno's home care workers. SEIU's secrecy, its false claims of victory, and its inability to scuttle the cuts here in California where it's all so easy-peasy are not much of an endorsement for Medina and SEIU's prospects in what Lerner calls "the more difficult regions where workers face more difficult obstacles."

The invading army was opposed by perhaps 150 insurgents, including fired former staff, nearly all volunteers, some paid with donations, and healthcare workers who came to Fresno on weekends and days off. I had the privilege of seeing these volunteers in action—long days, temperatures of 105 degrees, no SUVs, no hotel rooms, no air conditioning, no swimming pools, no promotions promised back home. They were a very brave bunch in the circumstances and considering such odds. The SEIU leaders, a big chunk of SEIU's top management, shipped out for Fresno duty—Regan, Medina, Henry, Gerry Hudson—ridiculed the volunteers. They seem to have a problem with the concept of sacrifice.

In the first count—the election results are contested—SEIU won by fewer than 200 votes out of 6,000 cast—not the slam-dunk that Regan predicted. Trustee Regan, Cornell grad Regan, had promised "an 'old school ass-whipping'" in Fresno. SEIU, he claimed, would "drive a stake through the heart of the thing that is NUHW," to "put them in the ground and bury them." Is this an Ivy League thing? SEIU with its $300 million annual budget outspent NUHW 50-to-1!

SEIU was able just to eke out a victory: a majority of fewer than 200, and there are still approximately 450 to 500 uncounted ballots to this day. Moreover, there are abundant allegations of SEIU misconduct, hardly surprising considering SEIU rhetoric, its management-like tactics and its bullying, slash and burn style. And this was just the beginning, a prelude to next year's crucial hospital elections. San Francisco writer, Randy Shaw compared SEIU's Fresno campaign to "carpet bombing" and the infamous Vietnam War General Curtis Lemay's strategy of "total war." The point here, Shaw asserted, is that "the campaign left its opposition unvanquished and likely better positioned than SEIU to win future elections." [117]

Predictably, the results of this SEIU "victory" were soon apparent. Fresno was evacuated; SEIU decamped, leaving a hollow shell behind; "It's just the way they do it," says Rosselli, "organize an election, count the votes, move on." [118] Then it begins all over again: mailings have begun, the robo-calls, radio spots, and so on.

The workers, quite rightly, were stunned and angry—none more so than those who voted for SEIU on the basis of the (false) claims that a NUHW victory would cost workers their contract, their hours, their wages. Sarah Jones, a Fresno long-term care provider, contends, "They ran their campaign based on threats, bribes, lies... They showed us an appalling disregard." Now these workers ask, and who wouldn't, "Where is SEIU?" But for the most part they get no response. [119] Flo Furman, 16 years a home care worker, a fired UHW steward and executive board member said of SEIU, "I have no idea what they're doing. I haven't heard anything at all from them. I don't even know who my rep is." Of course there is always the SEIU call center, that is, "Membership Resource Center": "Have you a question or a problem at work? Call 1-877." [120] Whoops, no Fresno number.

A footnote on Fresno: On November 6, 2009, NUHW accused the SEIU of changing ballots and threatening to report workers to immigration officials in a contentious battle to represent more than 10,000 home healthcare workers in Fresno County. NUHW filed the charges with the California Public Employment Relations Board. NUHW wants the board to throw out the results of the June election. "SEIU not only tolerated but encouraged people to break the law, intimidate people and harass people," said NUHW President Rosselli.

In a telephone interview, former SEIU employee Carlos Martinez said that he changed the ballots of healthcare workers after pressuring them to vote for SEIU. He said he was told to change the ballots by SEIU superiors. In written statements sent to the Public Employment Relations Board, employees said the SEIU pressured them to change their votes and then marked their ballots to reflect the change. The SEIU pressured workers by telling them they would lose their jobs, wages and benefits if they voted for the NUHW, Martinez said. They were also told, if they were illegal immigrants, that the NUHW wouldn't protect them from deportation like the SEIU had, he said. [121]

CHAPTER NINE

The Struggle Continues

The slog—the outcome SEIU leader Bill Ragen suggested in his first Iraq analogy—continues. SEIU remains up to its neck in this war with California healthcare workers.

Gloomy June dragged on. SEIU's troubles, it immediately became apparent, were far from finished. Another scandal. *PerezStern*, the website sympathetic to NUHW, asked, "What in the world would lead you to decide that you didn't have to bother paying your creepy outsourced security contractor?"[122] A very good question—one whose answer would inflict more damage on the current SEIU regime. It offered—and still does—a revealing window into the Stern regime: SEIU was taken to the U.S. District Court of San Francisco by security specialists the OSO Group, who charged them with breach of contract, fraud, negligent representation, allegedly for failing to pay $924,434.13, a portion of charges for services during the UHW "transition"—that is the period of the imposition of the trusteeship.

OSO is led by a former assistant U.S. attorney general. It lists a staff of former secret service agents, national and local law enforcement officers, and veterans of the armed forces. It specializes, among other things, in "counter-terrorism," and "intelligence and counter-intelligence." Court papers reveal that OSO was contracted to "provide substantial manpower to SEIU for security, protection and surveillance at various UHW facilities, including the UHW headquarters in Oakland..."

It is interesting that OSO was contacted well before SEIU's executive committee recommended trusteeship. OSO was to be responsible to "SEIU and its out-of-town leadership with twenty-four-hour, seven-day security, surveillance at various UHW facilities in California" as well as

> executive protection and drivers for the upper echelon of SEIU leadership visiting California during the UHW transition period ... including the provision of protection and privacy for SEIU executives involved in discreet meetings with CEO's of major hospital corporations and members of the California legislature... Between January 15 and January 20, 2009, the demand for manpower, security and protection services and drivers continued to increase exponentially at business facilities, hotels and private residences... the OSO Group established a command post at a hotel in Oakland...

OSO was essentially a highly paid security contractor at work for SEIU. It was hired for the same reasons Rumsfeld, Cheney, and Bush hired Blackwater: it provided a way for the new trustees to try to keep their hands clean. It is an example of the pervasive secrecy in SEIU culture; it goes hand in hand with the "discreet meetings" and back room handshakes preferred trustees by Regan, Medina and the rest of the SEIU "upper echelon."

One would have thought it best to pay these guys first! But it seems OSO was not at the head of the queue. Gonzalez, in the New York *Daily News*, reported that SEIU was deep in debt to the Bank of America—in total $87.7 million, including $10 million in loans in 2008 alone. Gonzalez asked, "So why would SEIU, which boasted nearly $250 million in dues income last year, even need to take out big loans from Bank of America and Amalgamated Bank? It turns out Stern's organization has been burning through cash."[123] It's been burn season in Californiraq! Where UHW members once contributed $30 million a year to SEIU ("to grow the union"), now this money is squandered, nowhere more so than in the war on NUHW.

Then, SEIU's bitter conflict with one time ally and partner UNITE HERE, came to a head—in a spectacular confrontation and a ferocious war of words. SEIU was accused of stealing thousands of UNITE HERE members (by supporting the UNITE group Workers' United, led by Bruce Raynor) plus millions in cash. A jurisdictional war began, with SEIU threatening to open a national campaign to win workers in UNITE HERE's jurisdictions—in hotels, casinos, airports, and other settings. Hugely ambitious, SEIU "will do anything to get dues," in the words of one-time foe, now SEIU ally, Rose Ann DeMoro of California Nurses Association (CNA), who called SEIU "a management surveillance team." This was all before negotiating the not-very-helpful (to anyone except CNA) jurisdictional agreement and truce with Stern's union.[124]

SEIU still openly seeks to dominate U.S. labor and the UNITE HERE escapade is by no means its first raid. But this time, perhaps, it has gone too far. The labor movement (and much of the progressive movement) looked away when SEIU raided the Puerto Rican teachers' union; it apparently found no fault in SEIU's backdoor bargains with politicians of all stripes—Pataki in New York, Schwarzenegger in California, Blagojevich in Illinois. The labor movement and its supporters were silent for the most part when SEIU wrecked UHW. Now, however, organized labor is aroused and it's about time. Almost the entire labor movement has united in defense of UNITE HERE and in opposition to Andy Stern and his regime in SEIU.

UNITE HERE is the union of hotel, food service, apparel and textile manufacturing, laundry, warehouse and casino gaming industries formed in a 2004 merger. It is a member of the SEIU-initiated and -dominated CtW federation. Now it is the apparent victim of a typical Stern maneuver—Raynor's faction of UNITE (leaders willing, members' views unknown) announced that they were leaving UNITE HERE to form "Workers' United" and join SEIU, all bought and paid for by SEIU. "Implosion," remember?

In response, top U.S. labor leaders attended UNITE HERE's June Convention in Chicago, a convention that, more than once, transformed itself into an anti-SEIU rally; these labor leaders joined delegates in condemning SEIU and Stern in terms unthinkable just months ago. If words could kill... Vince Giblin—president of the Operating Engineers, AFL-CIO—denounced Stern as "the Darth Vadar of the labor movement." [125] Terry O'Sullivan of the Laborers Union condemned the SEIU raid on UNITE HERE as "hijacking." Mike Casey, President of the San Francisco Labor Council and a UNITE HERE local president, called SEIU "the company union in our industry," adding that "we are battling both SEIU and the employers." In response to SEIU's call for arbitration in the dispute, delegates chanted, "They say arbitrate, we say incarcerate." UNITE HERE officials believe that the UNITE defectors, and ultimately SEIU, may be vulnerable to charges of a "criminal conspiracy to steal $23 million." Gerry McEntee, president of AFSCME, roared: this is "piracy on the high seas of organized labor" and "what the SEIU is doing is bullshit," then led the delegates in an extended chant, "Bullshit! Bullshit!" AFL-CIO leaders were joined by James Hoffa of the Teamsters and Joe Hansen of the United Food and Commercial Workers, both partners with SEIU in CtW. There were 12 international presidents in all. It was a dramatic and rare display of labor solidarity. At the same time, the presidents of more than 27 international unions published a letter pledging their support for UNITE HERE against SEIU's raids.[126]

Gonzalez called this a "seminal moment" in U.S. labor history: a host of leaders joining to condemn SEIU. Stern has "gone off the deep end," he concluded. "Change to Win is dead."[127]

John Wilhelm, the President of UNITE-HERE, declared that SEIU stood for "the suicide of the labor movement" and called the conflict "a fight with the boss's lackey union." "The boss's lackey union!" Whoa! Surely this must give us pause. This is an extraordinary charge, even with its vintage antecedents in labor. SEIU, they're saying, is "in bed with the boss." But isn't it SEIU that's meant to be the progressive? Didn't Lerner tell us that SEIU was "one of the most progressive and ambitious of a major union in recent history?"

At the UNITE HERE convention, in the presence of the AFL-CIO and CtW leaders, there was an unqualified rejection of the SEIU corporate model, with its shameless top-down paradigm, commandism, centralism, and antidemocratic rules and structures.

The UNITE HERE convention then took steps to:

- reform the union's constitution in response to the need for more transparency and accountability;
- create decision-making governing bodies of the union between conventions—known as the Executive Committee and the General Executive Board—that will now be composed of a voting majority who will be elected locally and regionally;
- constitute a new General Executive Board that will have greater power and accountability over the President and the other General Officers; and
- establish a "bill of rights" for union members and elected officers at local and international levels.

Wilhelm, in his concluding statement, proclaimed a new era: "I am proud of our Union's new constitution. It stands in stark contrast to the top-down, autocratic manner in which SEIU has approached our union and its own members. I believe that UNITE HERE is starting an exciting new chapter in our history, and I am proud to be part of a union that is led by its members." All to the good and to be supported. We need a challenge to "top-down" "autocratic" trade unionism… to "bosses' unions." And we need to open a new chapter.[128]

But thus far, it must be said that the real energy in the UNITE HERE story has concerned the issue of raiding. This is what brought out the old leaders, plus, to be fair, the widening antipathy to Andy Stern and his regime. Unions in the United States are enjoined to respect each other's turf. This is an issue with deep roots in labor going right back to the founding of the American Federation of Labor in 1886. And it is intimately connected to the principle of "union autonomy"—non-interference by "outsiders," union or otherwise, in internal union affairs. This last "principle" has commonly been the technical justification for watching in silence the lynching of UHW.

SEIU, as much as possible, continues to pretend that NUHW does not exist. But when its existence is acknowledged, SEIU unabashedly suggests that it, SEIU, is the victim, that in California NUHW is a "raider." Fletcher and Lichtenstein disagree; they explain: "… the fight between NUHW and SEIU is not a question of an old-fashioned 'raid.' [It is] instead a process which seeks to reestablish an ongoing, democratic, and highly successful trade union whose health and outlook is essential to any revitalization of trade unionism, on both a state and national basis."[129]

Absolutely. But there is another issue, a more central issue in the California struggle. And this is whether or not workers have a free choice of union? Or are they the property of a labor organization—to be organized and reorganized as its leaders see fit, traded around within SEIU like ball players in the desperate search for the championship team? And is this none of our business because it's "an internal matter?" More than 100,000 healthcare workers have petitioned to leave SEIU, only to be denied this right and held hostage by SEIU in colluding with the employers, the police, the courts, and the NLRB. SEIU has pulled out the stops to see that the labor board does not hold elections. It supports the Employee Free Choice Act, apparently, except if one happens to be an SEIU member.

The fact, then, is that there is more involved here than raiding, much more. And this is where NUHW returns to center stage. The California fight is also fundamentally about what kind of a labor movement we want—and need. The conflict, as Gonzalez has reported, is about "the soul of the labor movement."[130] And it is quite legitimate to ask the SEIU leaders "what are you? And which side are you on?"

We don't want "bosses' unions" and we don't need business unionism, whatever its current incarnation and we fear the ongoing decline and increasing irrelevance of organized labor. We want real democracy, participatory democracy. We don't want "discreet meetings" and backroom deals, no-strike agreements and ten-year contracts; we don't want thuggery and rent-a-mobs, we don't need Bolshevik centralism. We don't want what has happened in California.

We want unions with power, but unions that will fight for their members and all workers, on and off the job—for better wages and conditions but also, so important today, against foreclosures—for decent homes for people in a better world. We want, for the sake of the argument, what Kim Moody calls, "social movement unionism" or what labor activists and commentators Bill Fletcher Jr. and Fernando Gapasin call "social justice unionism."[131]

"Instead of creating a false dichotomy between 'organizing' and 'servicing,'" Steve Early argues in *Rebel Rank and File*,

> individual grievances are no less important than
> membership growth or grappling with other 'big
> picture' issues and challenges ... Real union power
> can only be created through democratic workplace
> organization, membership mobilization, strike
> activity, cross-border solidarity, and strong links
> between labor and other social movements.[132]

UHW—as far as I can see—was evidence that this "social unionism" is possible in our time. UHW was a well-organized, powerful, militant, progressive local union, 150,000 strong, led by its members. It didn't invent the wheel. But it fought for its members, supported other workers in struggle and was proud of its immigrant members; it opposed war abroad and fought for social justice at home. It was living testimony that another world is possible in the realm of workers, their organizations, and their lives.

UNITE HERE has the advantage of being an already established national union. It has the chance to defend itself legally, it has the opportunity to gain support from other unions and it has received support. It deserves it in this conflict. But the question remains, which way will it go from here?

Immediately following the Convention, Wilhelm, in a telephone news conference, was asked about NUHW and whether or not the embattled new union would receive UNITE HERE support. Wilhelm declared that NUHW was in fact the "harbinger" of the new direction; and that although the details remained to be worked out, support would come.

This support is critical, and this is not to belittle UNITE HERE's own great, but far from insurmountable, obstacles. These conflicts represent the central issues of the labor movement. Someone had to stand up to Stern's SEIU. "We didn't pick this fight," says Paul Kumar, one-time elected UHW vice president, "but it's a privilege to wage it." [133]

The California healthcare workers in UHW were clearing the way for others; they still are, though in astonishingly difficult circumstances. They were interrupted but, in NUHW, they are on the way back. At great cost to themselves, they led the first major rejection of the SEIU corporate perspective, a rejection utterly essential to any labor renewal. And they did this at a time when much of labor remained silent, cowed by SEIU triumphalism and its ever handy checkbook. Now this silence is being broken. Indeed the cracks in this silence are widening, thanks in no small part to the UNITE HERE fiasco, and the inexhaustible courage of the California healthcare workers.

Is the NUHW rebellion the harbinger of a new unionism? We hope so though there is nothing guaranteed. But it has already come a long way, and it is clear there is no going back. Its members are exceptional; their achievements thus far have been astonishing. But NUHW remains, of course, a work in progress.

What is at stake? Working class struggle has always been central to understanding reform and revolt in the history of capitalism; it has always been central to improving people's lives. Its presence, or absence, plays a fundamental role in the outcome of crises, nowhere more so than in the recessions and depressions that recur routinely. In the 1930s, the last period of general crisis, working class rebellion from below impelled the New Deal reforms from above—health and welfare programs, social security, the establishment of the rights of workers to organize collectively, to bargain, and to strike. In the social revolutions of the 1950s and 1960s, movements of black workers, again, from below, led the way in abolishing the legal system of racial segregation and in the process they helped vastly expand the boundaries of freedom, as well as opening the door for others—Latinos, women, youth, lesbians, and gays. And they integrated the labor movement, no small achievement.

In contrast, in today's crisis, the balance of forces has not shifted towards workers and social movements; it has instead favored those widely seen to be responsible for the catastrophe in the first place—hence we read of multi-million-dollar banker's bonuses, highly profitable financial and industrial readjustments and a recovery without jobs. So what is remarkable is the absence of a sustained working class response and the weakness of working class organization, in particular the failure of the trade unions to respond. In place of working class resistance, we witness retreat. In the unions, this has meant not only incapacity; we also see withdrawal into the worst features of business unionism and what Andy Stern refers to as "the political process"—that is the futile search for access and influence in Washington, D.C., encapsulated in SEIU's multi-million-dollar campaign contribution give-aways. All the while the union's internal regime is shored up in reaction to politicians' indifference and employers' intransigence. Yet, power, as we know, concedes nothing without demand. Thus, in these circumstances, working class Americans (nine out of ten of whom have no union at all) find themselves virtually defenseless, without a collective vision or voice, without effective organization and leadership—without the basis for collective action. This too, regrettably, will shape the form of the recovery.

The attack, then, on UHW, is all the more tragic—it also explains, in part, why this is an "employers' recovery." It is significant, then, far beyond the immediate needs of health-care workers—important as these are. UHW was a union driven by its members, a union without self-imposed limits on its vision—it fought for the standards of its members and supported progressive causes. Thus far its commitment to building from the bottom up, to empowering workers, its goal of a social union in a democratic society has been unshakeable. It was making great strides in shifting the balance of power in the healthcare industry. We still need a shift in that balance—and for all workers. We need to build unions, not wreck them. And not just in California. But that will take forces, real forces on the ground, and a vision of workers' power. Here, then, is the greater importance of the California healthcare workers—first, negative in removing UHW from the field, then positive in their struggle to rebuild their union, the NUHW, and the example their victory can mean for others. This is not to place the weight of the world on their shoulders—UHW was just one union in just one state; its capacities were by definition limited.

But already NUHW has won magnificent victories in a key series of electoral contests. In early January 2010 in the first elections allowed at Kaiser in Southern California, worker volunteers, health care workers managing their own campaigns, defeated SEIU-UHW by choosing NUHW in three crucial representational elections. Nurses at Kaiser-Sunset voted twenty-to-one for NUHW! Psychiatric and social workers and healthcare professionals voted NUHW by more than four-to-one.[134]

We need a labor *movement*, and what better place than NUHW to start. Its members are tough, their experience invaluable. They are fighters. And they are on our side. So our stake in the outcome of this conflict is great. It is an issue in which we all have much to gain and equally much to lose.

The prerequisite of unionism, the foundation on which any real labor movement is built, is solidarity. But solidarity raises the question, "Which side are you on?"—and it demands action. The campaigns of 2010, the hundreds of elections, are crucial. They demand support. The organized labor movement, with UNITE HERE thus far bravely in the lead, can follow the example and the generosity of the brothers and sisters in California, the trade unionists and labor leaders who stood with NUHW on November 16, 2009, at the Plumbers Hall in San Francisco. Progressives and reformers can follow the lead of *Labor Notes*, the rank-and-file network that has told NUHW's story and co-sponsored numerous receptions and fundraisers. Rank-and-file members can continue the struggle inside SEIU—in the belly of the beast, as it were. The chains that still bind the great majority of SEIU members must be smashed (borrowing a phrase from Rosa Luxemburg) where they have been forged.

We can all help. NUHW members need to be invited into our union halls, our community centers, our colleges and universities, into our kitchens and living rooms. NUHW needs support from organized labor, from political and community organizations, from individuals. It needs cash. Its members need the chance to tell their story.

"We had rights in UHW, they've taken them away," NUHW leader Angela Glasper says. "We fought for them; we won them. What is the use of having a union if it acts just the same as the company? SEIU, Kaiser, they're both against the workers. We won't stand for this. We don't need another boss, one is enough.

"I was born and raised in Tupelo, Mississippi. I've had to fight for my rights all my life. My shackles are off. I'm not going to stop now."[135]

APPENDIX I

May 1, 2008

Mr. Andrew Stern, President
Service Employees International Union
1313 L St. N.W.
Washington, D.C. 20005

Dear Andy,

We are writing to you as journalists, authors, political activists, and educators who are committed to organized labor because of its important role in social justice struggles in the U.S.

Some of us have longstanding ties to SEIU and have done research, writing, or labor education work involving its members, organizers, and local leaders. Those of us who deal with graduate students or undergraduates have encouraged younger people to pursue internships or fulltime job opportunities with SEIU and other Change To Win or AFL-CIO unions.

A number of us belong to unions ourselves. Many of us have been part of community-labor coalitions or campus-based groups like Scholars, Artists, Writers for Social Justice (when it was still active) because we support organizing and bargaining by janitors, cafeteria workers, and other service sector employees.

We are writing to express our deep concern about SEIU's threatened trusteeship over its third largest local, United Healthcare Workers (UHW). We believe that there must always be room within organized labor for legitimate and principled dissent, if our movement is to survive and grow.

Putting UHW under trusteeship would send a very troubling message and be viewed, by many, as a sign that internal democracy is not valued or tolerated within SEIU.

In our view, this would have negative consequences for the workers directly affected, the SEIU itself, and the labor movement as a whole.

We strongly urge you to avoid such a tragedy.

Sincerely,

Sara Abraham, Assistant Professor, Department of Sociology, University of Toronto
Michael Albert, Author, co-founder of South End Press and *Z Magazine*
Richard P. Applebaum, Professor of Sociology, Global and International Studies, UC Santa Barbara
Stanley Aronowitz, Professor of Sociology, CUNY Graduate Center
Frank Bardacke, Writer, Educator, and Former UFW Activist
Rosalyn Baxandall, Chair, American Studies, SUNY College at Old Westbury
Jennifer Berkshire, Editor, AFT Massachusetts Advocate
Elaine Bernard, Labor and Worklife Program, Harvard Law School
Fred Block, Dept of Sociology, University of California Davis
Edna Bonacich, University of California Riverside
Eileen Boris, Hull Professor and Chair, Women's Studies, University of California, Santa Barbara
Johanna Brenner, Professor of Sociology/Women's Studies, Portland State University
Robert Brenner, Professor of History, UCLA
Kate Bronfenbrenner, Cornell ILR School
Dan Brook, Department of Sociology, San Jose State University
Michael Jacoby Brown, Founder, Jewish Organizing Initiative, Lead Organizer/Director, MICAH, Framingham, MA
Anita Chan, Contemporary, Australian National University
Noam Chomsky, Professor of Linguistics (Emeritus), MIT
Levon Chorbajian, Professor of Sociology U-Mass, Lowell
Dan Clawson, Professor of Sociology, U-Mass Amherst
Bruce Cohen, Associate Professor of History, Worcester State College
Tim Costello, Labor Researcher and Author
Ellen David-Friedman, Founder, Vermont Workers' Center, Former Director of Organizing, Vermont-NEA
Mike Davis, History Professor; University of California, Irvine
Michael Denning, Professor of American Studies and Director, Initiative on Labor and Culture, Yale University

Micaela di Leonardo, Professor of Anthropology and Performance Studies, Northwestern University

G. William Domhoff, Research Professor of Sociology, UC-Santa Cruz

Kate Driscoll, Penn State

Jill Esbenshade, San Diego State University

Peter Evans, University of California Berkeley

Tess Ewing, UMass Boston Labor Center

Rick Fantasia, Professor of Sociology, Smith College

Leon Fink, Professor of History, University of Illinois at Chicago

Richard Flacks, University of California Santa Barbara

Bill Fletcher, Co-founder, Center for Labor Renewal & Executive Editor, BlackCommentator.com

John Bellamy Foster, Professor of Sociology, University of Oregon

Harris Freeman, U-Mass Amherst Labor Center

Paul Frymer, Department of Politics, University of California Santa Cruz

Yoshie Furuhashi, MRZine

Bill Gallegos, Executive Director of Communities for a Better Environment

William A. Gamson, Professor of Sociology, Boston College and former American Sociological Association president

Zelda Gamson, Senior Associate, New England Resource Center for Higher Education

Erik S. Gellman, Department of History, Roosevelt University

Dan Georgianna, University of Massachusetts Dartmouth

Sam Gindin, Packer Chair in Social Justice, York University; former Research Director & Assistant to the President, Canadian Auto Workers

George Gonos, Sociology and Employment Relations, SUNY Potsdam SUNY Potsdam

Suzanne Gordon, Health Care Journalist & Author, National Writers Union/UAW

Jim Green, Professor of History and Labor Studies, U-Mass Boston

Brian Greenberg, Department of History and Anthropology, Monmouth University

Nancy A. Hewitt, Professor of History and Women's & Gender Studies, Rutgers University

David Himmelstein, Harvard School of Public Health and Physicians for a National Health Program

Michael Honey, Professor of Humanities, University of Washington, Tacoma

Thandabantu Iverson, Assistant Professor in Labor Studies, Indiana University

Temma Kaplan, Professor of History, Rutgers, the State University of New Jersey

Robin D. G. Kelley, Professor of History and American Studies, USC

Brian Kelly, Senior Lecturer in U.S. History, Queen's University Belfast

Howard Kimeldorf, University of Michigan

Jennifer Klein, Department of History, Yale

Kitty Krupat, CUNY

Nelson Lichtenstein, Professor of History, Director of the Center for the Study of Work, Labor and Democracy, UC Santa Barbara

Stephanie Luce, Associate Professor, Labor Center, U-Mass-Amherst

Nancy MacLean, Professor of History, Northwestern University

Biju Mathew, Assistant Professor of Business, Rider University

Dale Melcher, UMass Labor Extension

Tom Mertes, Center for Social Theory and Comparative History, UCLA and Instructor, UCLA Extension

Jack Metzger, Emeritus Professor of Humanities, Roosevelt University

James Monsonis, Professor Emeritus, Simon's Rock College

David Montgomery, Farnam Professor of History Emeritus, Yale University

Carolina Bank Munoz, Assistant Professor of Sociology, Brooklyn College-CUNY

Ruth Needleman, Professor of Labor Studies, Indiana University

Manny Ness, Brooklyn College, City University of New York

Frances Fox Piven, CUNY Graduate Center

Vijay Prashad, Trinity College

Melvin H. Pritchard, History Instructor, West Valley College

Peter Rachleff, Professor of History, Macalester College

Marcus Rediker, Professor History, University of Pittsburgh

Adolph Reed, Professor of Political Science, Univ. of Pennsylvania

Thomas Reifer, Assistant Professor, Sociology and Ethnic Studies, University of San Diego

Christopher Rhomberg, Yale University

Corey Robin, Associate Professor of Political Science, Brooklyn College and the Graduate Center, CUNY

Ian Robinson, University of Michigan

Daisy Rooks, Rutgers University

Cesar F. Rosado-Marzon, Chicago-Kent College of Law

Lucy Rosenblatt, Psychotherapist, Health Workers for People Over Profits

Robert J.S. Ross, Professor Sociology, Clark University
Andrew Ross, New York University
Jay Schaffner, Author and Moderator, Portside
Michael Schwartz, SUNY Stony Brook
Robert Schwartz, Author and Attorney
Kathleen C. Schwartzman, Department of Sociology, University of Arizona
Kim Scipes, Assistant Professor of Sociology, Purdue University North Central
Dennis Serrette, President, United Association for Labor Education
Rae Sovereign, Labor Studies Program, Indiana University-South Bend
Chris Spannos, Znet/Z Communications
Judith Stepan-Norris, University of California Irvine
Zaragosa Vargas, Professor of History, University of California, Santa Barbara
Alan Wald, H. Chandler Davis Collegiate Professor, University of Michigan
Richard Walker, Chair, California Stuidies Center, Professor Geography, UC Berkeley
Immanuel Wallerstein, Professor of Sociology, Yale
Victor Wallis, Berklee College of Music, AFT Local 4412
Daniel J. Walkowitz, New York University
Andrea S. Walsh, Lecturer, Writing and Humanistic Studies, MIT
Dorian Warren, Columbia University
Eve Weinbaum, University of Massachusetts Amherst
Suzi Weissman, Professor of Politics, Saint Mary's College of CA
David Wellman, Professor of Sociology, University of California, Santa Cruz
Cal Winslow, Environmental Politics, UC Berkeley
John Womack, Professor, Department of HIstory, Harvard
Steffie Woolhandler, Harvard School of Public Health and Physicians for a National Health Program
Michael D. Yates, Professor Emeritus, University of Pittsburgh
Dr. Quentin Young, PNHP
Maurice Zeitlin, Department of Sociology, UCLA
Howard Zinn, Professor of History (Emeritus), Boston College
Michael Zweig, State University of New York at Stony Brook

See http://www.beyondchron.org/news/index.php?itemid=7622#more

Fred Ross, Jr.

Open letter to Workers at Santa Rosa Memorial Hospital

Why do SJHS and SEIU Fear a Free and Fair Election?

December 8, 2009

I met some of you for the first time in December 2004 at a rally with United Farm Workers co-founder Dolores Huerta, when she joined your call for St. Joseph Health System (SJHS) to negotiate ground rules for a free and fair election process. For the next four years, as an SEIU international organizer, I worked with you to build a powerful campaign that, by the fall of 2008, had convinced SJHS to sit down and negotiate.

But in March 2009, after ten years, I decided to leave SEIU. The tipping point came when I learned in February that the international union had decided in August 2008 to withdraw support for your campaign. This was at a critical moment. We had conducted our week of action in Orange County in July of that year at the SJHS motherhouse, and won unprecedented national publicity.

How did I find out that SEIU had withdrawn support for you when you needed it most? Last February, SEIU leaders from Washington took over its California healthcare local, SEIU-UHW. The campaign was suspended. Days later, over 200 SRMH workers were informed of impending layoffs. I offered to fight the layoffs alongside an experienced organizer who had spent two years on the campaign. However, this organizer was told by the new SEIU-UHW leadership, installed by Andy Stern, that SRMH workers were *no longer a priority.*

Several days later, a national leader of SEIU told me that SEIU could probably get a free and fair election agreement from SJHS by that June. I was shocked by what he admitted next: that the international union made a decision in August 2008 no longer to support workers at SJHS or put pressure on the system, because they did not want you to have the opportunity to vote for a union led by Sal Rosselli. SEIU broke faith and trust with you by deserting you when you most relied on them. This misconduct seriously undermined the opportunity you had to win a fair election agreement with SJHS in the fall of 2008.

Later in February, the international union learned that many of you had decided to form a union with NUHW. SEIU made a last-ditch appeal that I lead a campaign to win your trust. Because of SEIU's breach of faith, I could no longer represent SEIU in good conscience.

I was disappointed but not surprised when SEIU rejected the offer of former Secretary of Labor Robert Reich and Monsignor Brenkle to mediate a fair election agreement, while NUHW accepted. Both SEIU and SJHS fear that if you have a free and fair election process with no intimidation, retaliation, or negative campaigning you will vote your conscience and select NUHW: the union whose leaders have stood by you for the past six years. SEIU's actions have had the effect of encouraging SJHS to mount a very aggressive anti-union campaign.

SEIU'S TRACK RECORD

SEIU has raised the issue of track record, so it is only fair to review its own recent track record. SEIU President Andy

Stern is currently embroiled in costly, divisive battles on several fronts. He is waging a union-busting campaign against the union representing his own employees; he is fighting and raiding his former ally, UNITE HERE.

SEIU is bogged down in conflicts of its own making at a time when the labor movement has a once in a lifetime opportunity to make historic gains with the Obama Administration and a Democratic Congress. And now the labor movement is being tarnished, as numerous Stern proteges and appointees have been forced to resign amidst charges of rampant corruption.

Sadly, SEIU has chosen war with the former leaders of one of the most vibrant and successful healthcare unions in the country. Dissent has become equated with disloyalty.

SEIU once the fastest growing union in the United States has hit a wall. It has abandoned organizing campaigns at five major health systems around the country, after spending tens of millions of dollars, leaving pro-union activists vulnerable to management retaliation.

THE NEW SEIU: INTIMIDATION, THREATS, COERCION AND EVEN PHYSICAL VIOLENCE

Across California, prominent local leaders are joining in support of NUHW, because they know this California-based and member-led union will fight the hardest for healthcare workers. Sterns trustee for SEIU-UHW, Dave Regan, has failed in his attempt to threaten and coerce Local 2 UNITE HERE President Mike Casey into withdrawing his support for NUHW.

When SEIU tried the same bullying tactics on John Burton, California Democratic Party Chair and legendary champion of working people, it backfired. Burton publicly supported the character, integrity and leadership of Sal Rosselli. But SEIU reached a new low when it resorted to physical violence against the Vice President of the United

Teachers of Los Angeles (UTLA) and other labor supporters of NUHW at a recent event in Los Angeles.

Not surprisingly, significant numbers of very talented staff have left SEIU. This represents a talent and idealism drain in the union that once was a beacon for idealistic young people.

YOUR CHOICE

The danger, of course, is that your co-workers become discouraged and vote for neither union. It has been 39 years since I went to Delano to work for César Chávez. I helped organize the successful campaign to defeat the all-powerful Teamsters in the 1970s.

Today you have an historic opportunity to cast your vote for NUHW, whose leaders have a long and proud track record of building a member driven union that has won voice in patient care, respect, and the highest benefits of any healthcare union west of the Mississippi. NUHW is organized and led by the people you know and trust. Workers in over 80 healthcare facilities and systems in California are in the process of joining NUHW because they want a union that they control themselves.

Keep your eyes on the prize. You can withstand SJHS's anti-union campaign. You will overcome SEIU's campaign of smear, fear and futility. By voting for NUHW, Memorial Employees will have the voice you need and deserve for yourselves and your patients. It will also send a powerful message to SJHS and SEIU and inspire workers in the rest of SJHS and in Catholic hospitals across this country.

Fred Ross, Jr. is an organizer for IBEW 1245 and a longtime supporter of UNITE HERE Local 2.

NOTES

This story is very well documented. Much of this reporting originally appeared in *CounterPunch*. NUHW, SEIU and UNITE HERE have all websites posted extensively. Before trusteeship, the best source was *SEIU-VOICE*, the UHW website. The most interesting source was *PEREZSTERN*, a site of pro-NUHW activists that lasted from February to October 2009. The full report of the Marshall Commission can be found on the SEIU website. In addition I personally observed many of the events described here and have interviewed scores of UHW-NUHW members and leaders, hence my notes are the source of many quotations, etc. Steve Early, who also covered this story firsthand, allowed me access to interviews and notes, which I have used freely.

1   See, for example, C. Wright Mills, *The New Men of Power* (New York: Harcourt, Brace, 1948).

2   Kim Moody, *An Injury to All* (New York: Verso, 1988), 20.

3   Calvin Winslow, ed., *Waterfront Workers* (Champaign: Illinois, 1999) 62-96.

4   See Cal Winslow, et al., ed., *Rebel Rank and File* (New York: Verso, Spring 2010)

5   "California Unemployment Rate Hits 12.2 percent in August," *Los Angeles Times*, September 19, 2009.

6   Juan Gonzalez, "SEIU Goes to the Extreme," *Daily News*, March 25, 2009.

7   Some receive token wages and benefits thanks to donations.

8   *Wall Street Journal*, October 30, 2009.

9   Harold Meyerson, "Labor's real Fight," *Los Angeles Times*, February 1, 2009.

10 Steve Early, "A Purple Uprising in Oakland, *CounterPunch*, April 2, 2008.

11 Report and Recommendations to the International President, *SEIU.org/images/pdfs/hearingofficerreport*, "Ray Marshall," January 21, 2009, 23.

12 "Las Vegas Meeting," *SEIU-Voice*, January 5, 2009. Report in author's possession.

13 *SEIU.org/a/ourunion/trusteeship-document*, UHW Ex 115.

14 "An Open Letter to Andrew L. Stern", November 16, 2008 (California elected officials and community leaders).

15 Steve Early, *Embedded with Organized Labor* (New York: Monthly Review, 2009), 254.

16 Report and Recommendations to the International President, "Ray Marshall," *SEIU.org/images/pdfs/hearingofficerreport*, January 21, 2009.

17 Stern letter to Rosselli, *SEIU.org/a/ourunion/trusteeship-document*, March 24, 2008. UHW Ex 018.

18   Report and Recommendations to the International President, "Ray Marshall," *SEIU.org/images/pdfs/hearingofficerreport*, January 21, 2009.

19   "Platform for Change," *SEIU.org/a/ourunion/trusteeship-document*, UHW Ex 035.

20   Michael D. Yates, David Bacon, Warren Mar, Stephen Lerner, and John Borsos, "SEIU: Debating Labor's Strategy," *MRZine*, July 14, 2008.

21   Ibid.

22   Herman Benson, "Reflections on the SEIU Convention in Puerto Rico," *Union Democracy Review* (2008), 174.

23   David Moberg, "Dissent in the Ranks," *In These Times*, April 9, 2008.

24   Michael D. Yates, David Bacon, Warren Mar, Stephen Lerner, and John Borsos, "SEIU: Debating Labor's Strategy," *MRZine*, July 14, 2008.

25   Ibid.

26   "On the Record: Sal Rosselli," *San Francisco Chronicle*, May 29, 2005.

27   Liza Featherstone, *Nation*, July 16, 2007.

28   Bob Hebert, "They Still Don't Get It," *New York Times*, January 22, 2010.

29   Steve Early, "SEIU Civil War Puts 'Partnership' in New Light," review of Kochan, McKersie, Eaton and Adler, *Healing Together: The Labor management Partnership at Kaiser Permanente*, in *Dollars and Sense* (September/October 2009)

30   "The California Alliance Agreement: Lessons Learned in Moving Forward in Organizing California's Nursing Home Industry," *SEIU. org/a/ourunion/trusteeship-document*, UHW Ex 006.

31   Ibid.

32   Jamie Court, President, Consumer Watchdog, author's note.

33   David Moberg, *In These Times*, October 24, 2007.

34   Ibid.

35   "The California Alliance Agreement: Lessons Learned in Moving Forward in Organizing California's Nursing Home Industry," *SEIU. org/a/ourunion/trusteeship-document*, UHW Ex 006.

36   Michael D. Yates, David Bacon, Warren Mar, Stephen Lerner, and John Borsos, "SEIU: Debating Labor's Strategy," *MRZine*, July 14, 2008.

37   "SEIU Healthcare Organizing: A Report on Issues Related to Growth and Density," *oneunitehere.org*, March 19, 2009.

38   David Moberg, *In These Times*, October 24, 2007.

39   Juan Gonzalez, "Union Fights over Bank," New York *Daily News*, February 20, 2009.

40   Kris Maher, "Unions Forge Secret Pacts," *Wall Street Journal*, May 10, 2008.

41   Steven Greenhouse, "Union Grows, but Leader Faces Criticism," *New York Times*, February 29, 2008.

42   John Borsos, "SEIU: Debating Labor's Strategy," *MRZine*, July 14, 2008.

43   Rosselli interview with author.

44   Michael D. Yates, David Bacon, Warren Mar, Stephen Lerner, and John Borsos, "SEIU: Debating Labor's Strategy," *MRZine*, July 14, 2008.

45 Andy Stern, *A Country That Works* (New York: Free Press, 2006), 70–71.

46 Matt Smith, "Union Disunity," *SF Weekly*, April 11, 2007.

47 Sal Rosselli, Letter to Stern and Burger, June 1, 2007, *SEIU.org/a/ourunion/trusteeship-document*, UHW Ex 016.

48 *Capitol Weekly*, December 6, 2007.

49 *San Francisco Chronicle*, February 17, 2008.

50 *San Francisco Chronicle*, March 27, 2008.

51 Steven Greenhouse, *New York Times*, April 16, 2008.

52 Ibid.

53 "Attention SEIU President Andy Stern," *New York Times*, May 3, 2008.

54 Andy Stern, "Dear Educators," May 2, 2008.

55 Eliseo Medina and Gerry Hudson, "Dear Educators," May 5, 2008.

56 Michael D. Yates, David Bacon, Warren Mar, Stephen Lerner, and John Borsos, "SEIU: Debating Labor's Strategy," *MRZine*, July 14, 2008.

57 Andy Stern, "Dear Educators," May 2, 2008. See also 47 local leaders, "Dear Educators," May 5, 2008.

58 Steve Early, "The Progressive Quandary About SEIU", *WorkingUSA*, November 23, 2009.

59 Ibid.

60 Paul Krehbiel, "NUHW Supporters Brave Eggs, Bottles," *Labor Notes*, November 18, 2009.

61 Herman Benson, *bensonsblog.blogspot/2009/09/new-constitution-for-unite-and-for-html*.

62 *SEIU-Voice* (author's notes)

63 Charlene Harrington, "To Whom it May Concern," letter on UCSF stationery, dated July 9, 2008, exhibit in Marshall Report.

64 Paul Pringle, "Tyrone Freeman Steps Aside as Head of SEIU Chapter," *Los Angeles Times*, August 21, 2008.

65 Paul Pringle, "Service Union Bans Former California President for Life," *Los Angeles Times*, November 27, 2008.

66 Paul Pringle, "SEIU Leader Loses Post over Scandals," *Los Angeles Times*, October 16, 2009.

67 Paul Pringle, "Top SEIU Official in California Quits Three Posts," *Los Angeles Times*.

68 *SEIU.org/a/ourunion/trusteeship-document*, UHW EX 060.

69 *Democracy Now!* September 19, 2008.

70 Author's notes.

71 Dan Clawson, "SEIU: The Members Weigh In," draft quoted with author's permission.

72 *SEIU-Voice* (website taken down) report in author's possession.

73 *SEIU-Voice* (website taken down) report in author's possession.

74 Steve Early and Cal Winslow, "Can SEIU Members Exorcize the Purple Shades of Jackie Presser?" *CounterPunch*, September 3, 2008.

75 Stephen Greenhouse, "Union Seeks Stronger Ethics Rules Amid Scandals," *NY Times*, September 2, 2008.

76   Steve Early interviews.

77   Report and Recommendations to the International President, "Ray Marshall," *SEIU.org/images/pdfs/hearingofficerreport*, January 21, 2009.

78   Steve Early,"Who Rules SEIU," *CounterPunch*, January 5, 2009.

79   Author's notes.

80   This chapter is a revised version of Cal Winslow, "Stern Gang Seizes UHW Union Hall", *CounterPunch*, February 2, 2009.

81   Dan Clawson, "SEIU: The Members Weigh In," draft quoted with author's permission.

82   Victoria Colliver, "Kaiser Earnings Up 30 percent," *San Francisco Chronicle*, February 16, 2007. *Fortune*, "The 35 largest Companies," *Money.cnn.com*

83   "SEIU United Healthcare Workers-West, On the Record: Sal Rosselli," *SFGate.com*, May 29, 2005.

84   Angela Glasper interview with author.

85   Author's convention notes.

86   Andy Stern, *USA Today*, March 22, 2009.

87   Mell Garcia, interview with author.

88   Evelyn Larrubia, "Bay Area Health Union seeks Vote on Membership," *Los Angeles Times*, February 3, 2009

89   Ibid.

90   *San Francisco Chronicle*, March 19, 2009.

91   Incidents compiled by Fred Seavey.

92   Steve Early, "Checking Out of Stern's Hotel California," *CounterPunch*, February 2, 2009.

93   Ibid.

94   Ibid.

95   Ibid.

96   See for example, Ruth Milkman and Kim Voss, *Rebuilding Labor: Organizing and Organizers in the New Union Movement* (Ithaca: Cornell, 2004) and Kim Voss and Rick Fantasia, *Reorganizing the Rust Belts* (Berkeley: UC Press, 2004). Ruth Milkman (Editor)

97   Program, "Challenging Corporate Control: A Labor Teach-in at Yale University," April 16–18, 1999. My emphasis.

98   Steve Fraser, "Is Democracy Good for Unions," *Dissent* 45 (1998).

99   Stanley Aronowitz, "Unions and Democracy," *Dissent* 46 (1999).

100 Matt Witt and Rand Wilson, "The Teamsters' UPS Strike of 1997: Building a New Labor Movement," *Labor History Journal* 24 (1999): 58.

101 Steven Greenhouse, "Union Grows, but Leader Faces Criticism," *New York Times*, February 29, 2008.

102 Matthew Kaminski, "Let's Share the Wealth," *Wall Street Journal*, December 6, 2008.

103 Kim Moody, *U.S. Labor in Trouble and Transition* (New York: Verso, 2007), 184.

104 "Union, Nursing Home Alliance Team Up," *Seattle Times*, March 5, 2007.

105 Juan Gonzalez, "New York Labor Leader Dennis Rivera in Shady Puerto Rico Union Deal," New York *Daily News*, February 29, 2008.

106 Paul Pringle, "A Year of Triumphs and Scandals for SEIU," *Los Angeles Times*, December 31, 2008. "SEIU President Says He Will Seek Aid from Union Reform Groups, *Los Angeles Times*, September 6, 2008.

107 Herman Benson, "Hybrid Unionism," *Dissent* (Winter 2009).

108 Randy Shaw, "Progressive Outpouring for Rosselli," *BeyondChron*, November 19, 2008.

109 Deloros Huerto, *AdiosAndy.blogspot.com*, May 28,2009.

110 An Open Letter to Andy Stern from California Educators, Writers, Artists, and Trade Unionists, October 2008.

111 Kris Maher, "Illinois Scandal Spotlights SEIU's User of Politics," *Wall Street Journal*, December 20, 2008.

112 Eileen Boris and Jennifer Klein, "Organizing Home Care: Low-Waged Workers in the Welfare State," *Politics and Society* 34, no. 1 (2006): 82.

113 Eliseo Medina, email correspondence with author. Michael D. Yates, David Bacon, Warren Mar, Stephen Lerner, and John Borsos, "SEIU: Debating Labor's Strategy," *MRZine*, July 14, 2008.

114 Alan Berube, "Confronting Concentrated Poverty in Fresno," *Brookings.edu*, September 6, 2006.

115 American Lung Association, "10th Annual State of the Air report," *lungusa.org*, April 29, 2009.

116 Bureau of Labor Statistics,"Overview of BLS Statistics on Unemployment," *bls.gov*, December 2009.

117 Randy Shaw, "Is Fresno SEIU's Vietnam?" *BeyondChron*, June 22, 2009.

118 Rosselli, interview with author.

119 Sarah Jones, interview with author.

120 Flo Furman, interview with author.

121 Fresno Bee, November 12, 2009.

122 National Legal and Policy Center, "SEIU Hires Union Busting Security Firm to Aid in California Trusteeship," May 13, 2009.

123 Juan Gonzalez, "SEIU President Andy Stern has been Bashing Bank of America, the Same Bank that Gave Union a Big Loan," New York *Daily News*, April 30, 2009.

124 Randy Shaw, "The Shocking SEIU-CNA Alliance," BeyondChron, March 20, 2009. *CNA.org*, January 28, 2009.

125 Steven Greenhouse, "Infighting Distracts Unions at Crucial Time," *New York Times*, July 9, 2009.

126 Randy Shaw, "Labor Movement Backs UNITE HERE Against SEIU Raids," *BeyondChron*, June 30, 2009.

127 Juan Gonzalez, "Change to Win is Dead," *Democracy Now!* July 1, 2009.

128 Pilar Weiss, UNITE HERE Press Release, June 30, 2009.

129 Bill Fletcher, Jr. and Nelson Lichtenstein, "SEIU's Civil War," *In These Times*, December 16, 2009.

130 Juan Gonzalez, "SEIU President Andy Stern is a Threat to Labor Soul," New York *Daily News*, December 31, 2008.

131 Bill Fletcher, Jr. and Fernando Gapasin, *Solidarity Divided* (Berkeley, UC Press, 2008).

132 Steve Early, *Rebel Rank and File* (New York: Verso, forthcoming)

133 Paul Kumar, interview with author.

134 Cal Winslow, "Healthcare Workers Savor a Victory," *CounterPunch*, February 5, 2010.

135 Angela Glasper, interview with author.

ABOUT THE AUTHOR

Cal Winslow, PhD, is an historian, trained at Warwick University under the direction of the late E.P. Thompson. He is a co-author, along with Thompson and others of *Albion's Fatal Tree*. He is a fellow in Environmental Politics at UC Berkeley and the Director of the Mendocino Institute. He is associated with the Bay Area collective, Retort and is co-editor of *Rebel Rank and File, Labor Militancy in the Long Seventies* (Verso). He lives with his family on the Mendocino Coast. His daughter, Samantha Winslow, worked as an organizer for UHW from 2004 through 2009; as a staff member she was a founder of NUHW.

ABOUT PM PRESS

PM Press was founded at the end of 2007 by a small collection of folks with decades of publishing, media, and organizing experience. PM co-founder Ramsey Kanaan started AK Press as a young teenager in Scotland almost 30 years ago and, together with his fellow PM Press co-conspirators, has published and distributed hundreds of books, pamphlets, CDs, and DVDs. Members of PM have founded enduring book fairs, spearheaded victorious tenant organizing campaigns, and worked closely with bookstores, academic conferences, and even rock bands to deliver political and challenging ideas to all walks of life. We're old enough to know what we're doing and young enough to know what's at stake.

We seek to create radical and stimulating fiction and non-fiction books, pamphlets, t-shirts, visual and audio materials to entertain, educate and inspire you. We aim to distribute these through every available channel with every available technology - whether that means you are seeing anarchist classics at our bookfair stalls; reading our latest vegan cookbook at the café; downloading geeky fiction e-books; or digging new music and timely videos from our website.

PM Press is always on the lookout for talented and skilled volunteers, artists, activists and writers to work with. If you have a great idea for a project or can contribute in some way, please get in touch.

PM Press
PO Box 23912
Oakland, CA 94623
www.pmpress.org

FRIENDS OF PM PRESS

These are indisputably momentous times—the financial system is melting down globally and the Empire is stumbling. Now more than ever there is a vital need for radical ideas.

In the year since its founding—and on a mere shoestring—PM Press has risen to the formidable challenge of publishing and distributing knowledge and entertainment for the struggles ahead. With over 75 releases to date, we have published an impressive and stimulating array of literature, art, music, politics, and culture. Using every available medium, we've succeeded in connecting those hungry for ideas and information to those putting them into practice.

Friends of PM allows you to directly help impact, amplify, and revitalize the discourse and actions of radical writers, filmmakers, and artists. It provides us with a stable foundation from which we can build upon our early successes and provides a much-needed subsidy for the materials that can't necessarily pay their own way. You can help make that happen—and receive every new title automatically delivered to your door once a month—by joining as a Friend of PM Press. Here are your options:

- **$25 a month** Get all books and pamphlets plus 50% discount on all webstore purchases
- **$25 a month** Get all CDs and DVDs plus 50% discount on all webstore purchases
- **$40 a month** Get all PM Press releases plus 50% discount on all webstore purchases
- **$100 a month** Sustainer—Everything plus PM merchandise, free downloads, and 50% discount on all webstore purchases

Your Visa or Mastercard will be billed once a month, until you tell us to stop. Or until our efforts succeed in bringing the revolution around. Or the financial meltdown of Capital makes plastic redundant. Whichever comes first.

In and Out of Crisis: The Global Financial Meltdown and Left Alternatives

Greg Albo, Sam Gindin, Leo Panitch

978-1-60486-212-6
160 pages
$13.95

While many around the globe are increasingly wondering if another world is indeed possible, few are mapping out potential avenues—and flagging wrong turns—en route to a post-capitalist future. In this groundbreaking analysis of the financial meltdown, renowned radical political economists Albo, Gindin and Panitch lay bare the roots of the crisis in the inner logic of capitalism itself.

With an unparalleled understanding of capitalism, the authors provocatively challenge the call by much of the Left for a return to a largely mythical Golden Age of economic regulation as a check on finance capital unbound. They deftly illuminate how the era of neoliberal free markets has been, in practice, under-girded by state intervention on a massive scale. The authors argue that it's time to start thinking about genuinely transformative alternatives to capitalism—and how to build the collective capacity to get us there. *In and Out of Crisis* stands to be the enduring critique of the crisis and an indispensable springboard for a renewed Left.

"Greg Albo, Sam Gindin, and Leo Panitch provide a perceptive, and persuasive, analysis of the origins of the crisis, arguing that the left must go beyond the demand for re-regulation, which, they assert, will not solve the economic or environmental crisis, and must instead demand public control of the banks and the financial sector, and of the uses to which finance is put. This is an important book that should be read widely, especially by those hoping to revitalize the left."
— Barbara Epstein, author of *The Minsk Ghetto 1941–1943: Jewish Resistance and Soviet Internationalism*

"The Left has often been accused of not understanding economics properly. So it's been no small pleasure over the last year to see the guardians of neo-liberal orthodoxy thrashing around helplessly in a bid to explain the financial meltdown... Leo Panitch has stood out in recent years as one of the socialist intellectuals most fully engaged with political questions, analyzing the problems faced by left-wing parties, trade unions and other social movements with great clarity."
— *Irish Left Review*

Capital and Its Discontents: Conversations with Radical Thinkers in a Time of Tumult
Sasha Lilley

978-1-60486-334-5
320 pages
$20.00

Capitalism is stumbling, empire is faltering, and the planet is thawing. Yet many people are still grasping to understand these multiple crises and to find a way forward to a just future. Into the breach come the essential insights of *Capital and Its Discontents*, which cut through the gristle to get to the heart of the matter about the nature of capitalism and its inner workings. Through a series of incisive conversations with some of the most eminent thinkers and political economists on the Left—including David Harvey, Ellen Meiksins Wood, Mike Davis, Leo Panitch, Tariq Ali, and Noam Chomsky—*Capital and Its Discontents* illuminates the dynamic contradictions undergirding capitalism and the potential for its dethroning. At a moment when capitalism as a system is more reviled than ever, here is an indispensable toolbox of ideas for action by some of the most brilliant thinkers of our times.

"These conversations illuminate the current world situation in ways that are very useful for those hoping to orient themselves and find a way forward to effective individual and collective action. Highly recommended."
— Kim Stanley Robinson, *New York Times* bestselling author of the *Mars Trilogy* and *The Years of Rice and Salt*

"This is an extremely important book. It is the most detailed, comprehensive, and best study yet published on the most recent capitalist crisis and its discontents. Sasha Lilley sets each interview in its context, writing with style, scholarship and wit about ideas and philosophies."
— Andrej Grubacic, radical sociologist and social critic, co-author of *Wobblies and Zapatistas*

"In this fine set of interviews, an A-list of radical political economists demonstrate why their skills are indispensable to understanding today's multiple economic and ecological crises."
— Raj Patel, author of *Stuffed and Starved* and *The Value of Nothing*

Global Slump: The Economics and Politics of Crisis and Resistance
David McNally

978-1-60486-332-1
176 pages
$15.95

Global Slump analyzes the world financial meltdown as the first *systemic* crisis of the neoliberal stage of capitalism. It argues that—far from having ended—the crisis has ushered in a whole period of worldwide economic and political turbulence. In developing an account of the crisis as rooted in fundamental features of capitalism, *Global Slump* challenges the view that its source lies in financial deregulation. It offers an original account of the "financialization" of the world economy and explores the connections between international financial markets and new forms of debt and dispossession, particularly in the Global South. The book shows that, while averting a complete meltdown, the massive intervention by central banks laid the basis for recurring crises for poor and working class people. It traces new patterns of social resistance for building an anti-capitalist opposition to the damage that neoliberal capitalism is inflicting on the lives of millions.

"In this book, McNally confirms—once again—his standing as one of the world's leading Marxist scholars of capitalism. For a scholarly, in depth analysis of our current crisis that never loses sight of its political implications (for them and for us), expressed in a language that leaves no reader behind, there is simply no better place to go."
— Bertell Ollman, Professor, Department of Politics, NYU, and author of
   Dance of the Dialectic: Steps in Marx's Method

"David McNally's tremendously timely book is packed with significant theoretical and practical insights, and offers actually-existing examples of what is to be done. Global Slump urgently details how changes in the capitalist space-economy over the past 25 years, especially in the forms that money takes, have expanded wide-scale vulnerabilities for all kinds of people, and how people fight back. In a word, the problem isn't neoliberalism—it's capitalism."
— Ruth Wilson Gilmore, University of Southern California and author,
   Golden Gulag

Labor Law for the Rank and Filer: Building Solidarity While Staying Clear of the Law
Staughton Lynd and Daniel Gross

978-1-60486-033-7
110 pages
$10.00

Labor Law for the Rank and Filer: Building Solidarity While Staying Clear of the Law is a guerrilla legal handbook for workers in a precarious global economy. Blending cutting-edge legal strategies for winning justice at work with a theory of dramatic social change from below, Staughton Lynd and Daniel Gross deliver a practical guide for making work better while re-invigorating the labor movement.

Labor Law for the Rank and Filer demonstrates how a powerful model of organizing called "Solidarity Unionism" can help workers avoid the pitfalls of the legal system and utilize direct action to win. This new revised and expanded edition includes new cases governing fundamental labor rights as well as an added section on Practicing Solidarity Unionism. This new section includes chapters discussing the hard-hitting tactic of working to rule; organizing under the principle that no one is illegal, and building grassroots solidarity across borders to challenge neoliberalism, among several other new topics. Illustrative stories of workers' struggles make the legal principles come alive.

"Workers' rights are under attack on every front. Bosses break the law every day. For 30 years Labor Law for the Rank and Filer *has been arming workers with an introduction to their legal rights (and the limited means to enforce them) while reminding everyone that real power comes from workers' solidarity."*
— Alexis Buss, former General Secretary-Treasurer of the IWW

"As valuable to working persons as any hammer, drill, stapler, or copy machine, Labor Law for the Rank and Filer *is a damn fine tool empowering workers who struggle to realize their basic dignity in the workplace while living through an era of unchecked corporate greed. Smart, tough, and optimistic, Staughton Lynd and Daniel Gross provide nuts and bolts information to realize on-the-job rights while showing us that another world is not only possible but inevitable."*
— John Philo, Legal Director, Maurice and Jane Sugar Law Center for Economic and Social Justice